THE FONIO COOK BOOK

THE FONIO COOK BOOK

AN ANCIENT GRAIN REDISCOVERED

BY PIERRE THIAM
PHOTOGRAPHY BY ADAM BARTOS

Lake Isle Press

Library of Congress Control Number: 2019942163
ISBN-13: 978-1-891105-69-2
ISBN-10: 1-891105-69-8

First edition
Printed in China

10 9 8 7 6 5 4 3 2 1

Published by:
Lake Isle Press, Inc.
2095 Broadway, Suite 301
New York, NY 10023
(212) 273-0796
info@lakeislepress.com

Distributed to the trade by:
National Book Network, Inc.
4501 Forbes Boulevard, Suite 200
Lanham, MD 20706
1(800) 462-6420
www.nbnbooks.com

Book and cover design: Pentagram,
Luke Hayman, Austin Maurer, Laura McNeill

Editors: Diana Kuan, Hiroko Kiiffner
Copyeditor: Suzanne Fass

This book is available at special sales discounts for bulk purchases
as premiums or special editions, including customized covers.
For more information, contact the publisher at (212) 273-0796 or
by e-mail: info@lakeislepress.com

To my love, Lisa, for dreaming with me.

Contents

Foreword

WHEN COOKING and eating become acts of sharing, food is no longer about nourishment, but about culture. Food can be elevated to this status only if we understand where it comes from. Cooking gives us the power to investigate things that are part of our primordial memory. Cooking has the potential to express who we are, and often it is food that helps us recall memories, emotions, and thoughts deeply rooted in our childhood. Each of us has a unique vocabulary of ingredients and flavors that circle our personal experiences. When we step outside of that known circle, we are often amazed to discover how limited our vocabulary is and how rich and diverse the world of flavor can be. Often this happens when I step into a chef's kitchen. This happened when I first met chef Pierre Thiam. He introduced me to an ingredient, a flavor, and a texture I had never tasted before: fonio. In *The Fonio Cookbook*, Pierre Thiam brings the culinary potential of this African grain to the table in an act of love and homage to the diverse cultural offerings of his Senegalese heritage.

Fonio is a perfect example of the importance of food research. One of the most compelling themes of food sustainability is elevating the potential of what we already have. Through this one ingredient, recipe after recipe, we are witness to talent, technique, and years of research that went into the formation of Thiam's culinary identity. He shares his rich African food culture through his contemporary kitchen and transfers emotion through his passion for his country of origin, Senegal, to the place where he is cooking today, Teranga at The African Center in Harlem.

When I recall my childhood memories, I find a never-ending source of culinary inspiration. I connect to another era, when "slow food" was just two words. I think about my grandmother in the kitchen, rolling out pasta dough, or my mother's red hands cleaning sour cherries to make my favorite jam. I am immediately transported to a place and time that grounds me and keeps me focused on the values that have always been part of my family. Today we are surrounded by an abundance of food information, and it is easy to disconnect from the emotional value of sharing a meal. Sharing a meal cooked with love and attention was something I almost took for granted, but as I have matured as a chef, I realized that it is the first thing a chef has to transmit: to infuse love, passion, and beauty into every meal. Then, and only then, can a chef create community through food.

Today, a chef has a responsibility to expand the role of cooking, to evolve from someone behind the saucepan to be a researcher, teacher, leader, and cultural conduit potentially cultivating sustainable systems that are precious for the planet and for people, and to promote cultural synthesis that is essential to our human biodiversity. This kind of culinary research elevates our purpose beyond making Good Food and draws a pathway for change, Food for Good. Chef Pierre Thiam has taken this courageous step beyond the four walls of the kitchen to bring this ancient grain with all of its health benefits, deliciousness, and cultural responsibility to the table for everyone to share.

—Massimo Bottura, Chef Patron of Osteria Francescana
    and Founder of Food for Soul

Introduction

BY 2050, there will be 10 billion inhabitants on Earth. How will we feed this rapidly growing world population without destroying our planet?

Modern agriculture has been great for mass production of food. It has helped fight famine, and allowed huge industries to be built across the world. But it's showing its limitations.

For one thing, it wasn't designed with the longevity of our planet in mind. Today's food production is causing approximately 30 percent of the world's greenhouse gas emissions. We use 70 percent of the available potable water on earth to grow our food.

While our palates are becoming more and more sophisticated—as is our consciousness about what we eat—the focus on large scale agriculture has also stripped us of the variety of foods that are readily available for consumption. Today, our global diet consists largely of four crops: corn, wheat, soy, and rice. Meanwhile, thousands of nutritious, resilient, planet-saving foods are simply being ignored. More than 90 percent of the planet's crop varieties have disappeared, and the lack of diversity in what we eat has given rise to worldwide health concerns.

What if we could find a way to use less water in agriculture? What if we could cause less damage to the earth while still eating foods we love? Right now, we have the opportunity to make some big changes in food production, water usage, the way we eat, and what we eat. And we have the power to live a healthier, more dynamic life.

Fonio, a tiny grain from an ancient culture, may hold clues as to how we can achieve these goals.

Why fonio?

You may wonder why a little-known ancient grain that grows in the Sahel region of West Africa is so significant that it deserves its own book. The answer is simple: Fonio can change the world.

Fonio is a delicious, nutritious health food alternative.

For those of you who have never heard of it, fonio is a tiny grain, roughly the size of quinoa, that is as versatile as rice or quinoa, and has a delicious, slightly nutty flavor. It's incredibly easy to cook, and difficult to get wrong—so much so that there is a popular Bambara saying that translates to "fonio never embarrasses the cook." Because it is light and easy to digest, fonio can be eaten alone or mixed with almost anything. When served with stews or gravies, it lusciously absorbs liquids, becoming moist and plump with each bite without losing its fluffiness.

In addition to its flavor and aroma, fonio also offers distinct nutritional benefits. It scores low on the glycemic index, which makes it less likely to cause large increases of blood sugar levels. Furthermore, fonio has particularly high amounts of methionine and cysteine, two amino acids that are essential for human growth and deficient in most other grains.

Fonio helps farming economies thrive.

Fonio is one of the world's fastest-growing edible grains. It is mainly grown in the dry and arid Sahel region of West Africa south of the Sahara desert, one of the poorest regions of the world. In this arid soil, not much can grow—but fonio thrives. It grows to maturity in two to three months, depending on the variety. This is important, because farmers can rely on having fonio when their reserves from last year's harvest are depleted and nothing else has grown in yet. For this reason, fonio is also called hungry season rice—the "hungry season" being the time in an agricultural cycle when the harvest is not yet ready and barns are mostly empty. But in fonio regions, around this time, stocks of fonio fill the barns. After the first rain, farmers simply broadcast the seeds over the fields by the handful. Once the seeds are planted, farmers wait for a couple of months, then return to harvest. It's that easy! Fonio is even nicknamed the lazy farmer's crop because of how easy it is to grow.

Fonio farmers often live in communities that are severely hit by desertification and a lack of job opportunities. Bringing fonio onto the global stage may help transform the West African economy. Making life less precarious in one of the world's most vulnerable areas can reduce the sense of desperation that leads people toward perilous ocean crossings or extremist violence.

Fonio is great for the environment.

Fonio is drought resistant and incredibly resilient, and—thanks to its deep roots—restores the topsoil and stores carbon dioxide from the atmosphere. It requires very little water and grows easily in poor soil without chemical pesticides, herbicides, or fertilizers. In a region threatened by desertification, fonio is nothing short of a miracle grain. Taking CO_2 out of the atmosphere and storing it in the soil has significant environmental benefits and is one small step toward slowing down climate change.

Fonio is food for the soul.

A discussion of fonio would be incomplete without considering its cultural relevance. Food is more than just nourishment for the body. In the fonio-growing countries, including Senegal where I'm from, eating is always a communal activity shared with loved ones.

Traditionally, our food is served in large bowls placed on straw mats. We sit around the bowl, on wooden benches or directly on the mat, and eat with our right hands or with spoons. We consider eating together around a communal bowl a sign of love and trust for the people sitting in the circle. Whenever fonio is served, it's another sign of honoring the guest, as fonio is also nicknamed *ñamu buur*, or "food for royalty."

So why is fonio so little known?

Here is the crazy thing: Although fonio has been around for over 5,000 years and is probably Africa's oldest cultivated grain, right now it is cultivated almost exclusively by smallholder farmers who grow it for their own consumption. Outside of these communities, fonio—unlike grains that have gone completely mainstream, like rice and corn—is still relatively unknown.

How could such an amazing grain be snubbed and relegated to substandard "peasant" food? The history of colonization in Africa may shed some light on this condescending attitude towards fonio.

Beginning in the late 19th century, colonial powers favored and promoted the cultivation of specific crops for the exclusive interest of their markets. This scheme resulted in the large-scale production of commodities such as peanuts in Senegal, cocoa and coffee in Côte d'Ivoire and Ghana, and tea in Nigeria, Cameroon, or Kenya. There were many such instances of implementing these monoculture policies, and they were often

done with much hype. We believed "What Comes from the West Is Best."

This attitude, of course, brought unfortunate consequences.

We Senegalese were introduced to leftovers of overprocessed rice, known as broken rice, by French colonizers who imported it from their territories in Indochina (today's Vietnam, Cambodia, and Laos). We chose the less-nutritious broken rice over our homegrown and more nutritious cereals such as fonio, millet, sorghum, and even our own homegrown rice.

Today, more than half a century after our so-called independence, this colonial mentality is still alive and well. We haven't truly developed an appreciation for our own crops, and we still rely on broken rice imports. The national government has been making efforts to promote production of local products in general, but rice in particular, and major rice-growing farms have been developed in the north of the country with government support. But other local grains are still not sufficiently promoted. We still prepare our national dish *thiebou jenn* —a boldly-flavored combination of fish, rice, and tomatoes—with broken rice. It is still much easier to find imported wheat products such as baguettes or croissants in the streets of Dakar or Abidjan than it is to find any fonio products.

The case of Senegal truly highlights the perversity of a colonial system that promoted cash over subsistence crops. We became one of the world's largest peanut producers, but at the same time we also became dependent on broken rice imports to feed ourselves. Ironically, these imports were likely paid for by money collected from peanut production. Furthermore, this intense monoculture of peanuts became a major factor in the degradation of our soils, which consequently brought desertification to the Sahel.

Before the agricultural colonization of Africa, fonio had a long and celebrated history on the continent. Arguably Africa's oldest cultivated cereal, it once formed part of the staple diet of great civilizations such as the ancient Egyptians and the Dogons of Mali. In these enlightened cultures, fonio had a revered status. To the ancient Egyptians, fonio was deemed worthy to be taken to the afterlife. It was among the sacred grains selected to be buried inside the tombs. To the Dogon people, fonio was considered the seed of the universe, the grain at the root of all existence. Nowadays, the Dogons still prepare fonio beer (see page 152) and eat fonio as porridge. Leaving little to waste, they combine leftover fonio straw with soil and water for use in construction.

Colonization is not the only reason fonio hasn't achieved widespread popularity. Transforming fonio into food is a tedious process and, until recently, was all done manually, using large wooden mortars and pestles carved out of mango tree trunks for hulling and calabash shells for washing. The difficulty in processing fonio, along with the colonizers' favoritism of new grains, made it scarce in most parts of Africa, and certainly in the world. Fonio's relatively unknown status, though, is beginning to change.

Today, in areas of West Africa where fonio is consumed, the grain's level of consumption is decidedly mixed. (Fonio production includes a vast swath of West Africa, from South Senegal through Guinea, Mali, Nigeria, Burkina Faso, Benin, Cameroon, Togo, Chad, and Ghana. In Guinea, Mali, Burkina Faso, and northern Nigeria, fonio is more of a staple; these countries are by far the largest producers and consumers of fonio. Fonio is cultivated in many other parts of West Africa in more localized, small-scale fields. In these regions, however, fonio is considered somewhat of a delicacy.

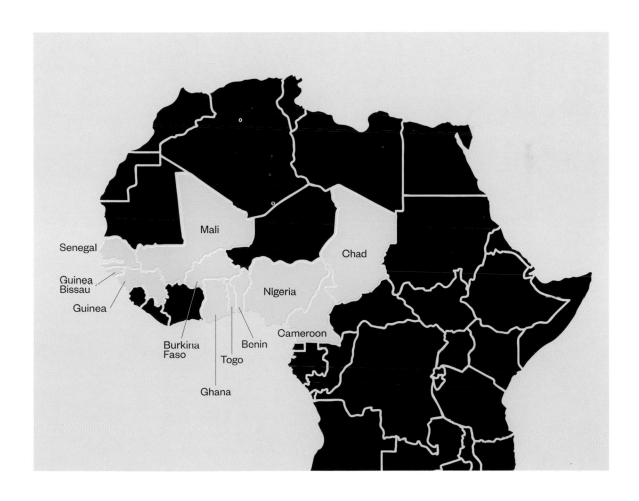

My story

I was born and raised in Dakar, the capital city of Senegal, while my parents are from the southern region of Casamance. Growing up, I only ate fonio during school summer breaks, while visiting my great-aunt Mamma in Kolda, a lush region in South Casamance on the border with Guinea.

Like Mamma, the majority of people living in Kolda are from the Fulani ethnic group, traditionally nomadic herders. In fact, they are the world's largest nomadic group. Many Fulanis still travel across the African continent with their cattle in search of pasture.

Like a growing number of Fulanis, however, Mamma never really lived the nomadic life of her ancestors. They became sedentary, abandoning their historically gypsy ways, choosing instead to become farmers—a lifestyle once considered an abomination. For them, fonio became the perfect crop of transition because of its ease of growth. Traditionally, Fulanis serve fonio on special occasions such as weddings or birth-naming ceremonies.

At Mamma's, we ate fonio the way others would eat rice. She often served it steamed, accompanied with a variety of offerings: a freshly pounded, bright red palm nut sauce; a generous and creamy peanut and root vegetable topping; a rich caramelized onion and lime relish; a red palm oil and sweet potato leaves stew; or a gooey okra sauce with lamb, fish, seafood, or vegetables. She also liked to serve it with *nététou*,[1] a spicy and pungent fermented condiment.

When the fonio was freshly harvested, Mamma would first toast the whole grains in a dry cast-iron pan placed on three stones or bricks over a fire pit, fueled with burning wood logs. Toasting fonio grains was optional, something Mamma would do only with freshly harvested grains for faster drying.

Once dried, fonio was easier to separate from its inedible hull, with the use of the ever-present mortar and pestle. Once the fonio was completely cleaned of its hull, Mamma would pound it once more into a thick paste and then sweeten it with local acacia honey. Behind the simplicity of this snack lay complex layers of flavors, from the smokiness imparted by the toasted grains to the unique sweetness of the acacia pollen.

Of course, the removed fonio hull didn't go to waste. Nothing ever went to waste in Mamma's kitchen. The fonio hull became animal feed for the chickens and ducks that lived in her backyard coop. At Mamma's, even the cold ash from the wood fire was recycled, mixed with a little water to make a thick paste to seal the narrow space between the top steamer pot of fonio and the bottom pot of boiling water, to prevent steam from escaping. (Mamma's steamer, by the way, looked like a large clay colander, the size of a wok.) Her fonio would always come out perfectly steamed, light and fluffy.

1   Nététou, also called *dawadawa*, is a fermented locust bean that tastes and looks like a darker version of the fermented Japanese soybean natto. As a kid, I didn't like the fermented smell of nététou, and since I was Mamma's favorite, she would keep it far away from my section of the bowl. However, I have now become a big fan of nététou and I always have some, dehydrated and tightly sealed in a glass jar, in my pantry.

2 Palm oil often plays
a dual role in many
cultures of the African
diaspora, as both food
and an offering for
traditional rituals. (In
my kitchen in New York,
when I don't have palm
oil, I use olive oil as a
substitute.)

Most often, she cooked fonio that had already been dried in the sun, in which case there was no need to toast it first before pounding to remove the hull. Mamma always steamed the cleaned fonio three consecutive times. Before the third steaming, she would gently fold finely chopped okra into the grains, making the fonio easier to swallow. Sometimes she would add powdered dried baobab leaves (also known as *lalo*), which has the same mucilaginous quality as okra and is often used as a thickener for sauces in Senegal. Other times, Mamma would simply add red palm oil.[2]

As a kid, summer vacations with my grandparents and aunts were my favorite food season. Mamma's favorite grains were millet or fonio. I loved the way she prepared fonio with a luscious lamb, peanut, and okra sauce. She would sit the large and colorful enamel bowl in the middle of a straw mat. The steamed fonio filled up the bottom of the bowl and in its center was the juicy lamb with the okra and peanut sauce.

How to eat fonio

Fonio preparation methods vary greatly across West Africa. One of my favorite ways of eating fonio—aside from the ways Mamma prepared it, of course—is in *djouka*, a dish from Mali. Here, fonio is mixed with ground peanuts, then steamed. Djouka can be eaten as is, as a snack, or with *tigadege* (peanut butter), or with tomato sauce and accompanied with various vegetables or meats, depending on the season. In the Guéra region of Chad, a variation of this dish is prepared using sesame seed paste as a substitute for the peanut paste.

Fonio can also be prepared as a porridge—the ultimate comfort food. In this case it is cooked with water in a pot instead of in a steamer, and stirred often with a wooden spoon until it has the consistency of thick polenta. Prepared this way, fonio porridge can be served with milk for breakfast or alongside a luscious sauce or stew.

I am particularly fond of *gwote acha*, the hearty fonio porridge from the Hausa people in northern Nigeria. It is reminiscent of risotto in texture and includes garden eggplant (small white eggplants that look like large eggs), tomatoes, cabbage, and sorrel leaves, and is spiced with Scotch bonnet peppers and amaranth grains. Gwote acha also comes with various cuts of meats, including tripe and liver.

Fonio can also be turned into portable snacks. Among my favorites are *fini ngomi* (Malian beignets prepared with fonio and sweet potato or banana) and savory vegetable and fonio fritters from Burkina Faso.

Cooking with fonio today

As a chef, I first became interested in fonio because of its delicate, nutty, and neutral flavor. Fonio dishes vary with the seasons. During hot summer months, I often serve fonio in salads with various summer vegetables, fruits, and herbs. One of my favorites is a fonio and mango salad, with cucumbers, heirloom tomatoes, and lots of mint and parsley. I serve the salad topped with crumbled spicy honey-glazed cashews and a lime vinaigrette. It's the perfect summer dish—fresh, light, fruity, herbaceous, spicy, and crunchy.

Come fall or winter, steamed fonio becomes a bed for rich sauces with either squash, cabbage, leafy greens, or root vegetables, often served with lamb, chicken, or even seafood. Fonio's subtle flavor makes it particularly well-suited for all styles of cuisines. It can replace any grain in your favorite recipes.

This book is an ode to a beautiful and important grain. It's also an invitation to explore and to be adventurous when cooking with fonio. Whichever recipes you pick, traditional or modern, there is no sin in personalizing them to your liking, as fonio is a forgiving grain. Just remember: "Fonio never embarrasses the cook."

Fonio History and Culture

WHEREVER it is cultivated, fonio—also known as *po* in Dogon country of Mali, *findi* in Senegambia, and *acha* in northern Nigeria—seems always to be connected with some form of myth or spirituality.

Over 5,000 years ago, the ancient Egyptians believed fonio was worthy of being taken into the afterlife. Fonio, along with other sacred grains, was selected to be buried with the deceased. The grains were expected to germinate once the tomb was sealed, and their growth symbolized the resurrection of the deceased.

The Egyptians were among the first to practice agriculture on a large scale. Thanks to the generous and periodic flooding of the Nile river, they developed complex irrigation methods that involved building basins for water management purposes. They cultivated a great diversity of vegetables, vines, and fruits in orchards and gardens. However, they had a particularly sacred devotion to the grains around which their diet revolved. Because it is one of the easiest grains to cultivate and the fastest to mature, it is likely that fonio was a staple in the ancient Egyptian diet.

According to hieroglyphs and pyramid wall drawings depicting elaborate banquets, ancient Egyptians had quite a sophisticated cuisine. Foie gras, pheasants, ducks, geese, bread, and all sorts of vegetables and wines were regular fare at the royal table.

I've often wondered how the pharaohs' chefs prepared fonio. Did they steam the grains, then fold it in finely chopped okra or palm oil, as we do in West Africa? Or did they have a different method of adding creaminess to the cooked fonio?

Fonio was also highly esteemed among the Dogons, another great civilization believed to be descendants of ancient Egyptians who migrated through Libya all the way to Mali. They called fonio *po*, or "the germ of the universe." In Kedougou, the fonio-growing region of Senegal that borders Dogon land, fonio is also called *ñamu buur*, which translates to "food for royalty."

Casamance, the southern area of Senegal where my family originated, has kept many of its cultural traditions despite the challenges of modernity. Some people in Casamance believe that growing fonio around one's house can protect the inhabitants from a bad spell or the evil eye. Newborn babies carry little pouches of fonio attached to their fists or ankles. Mothers wrap fonio in handkerchiefs, which they place in their kids' school belongings as lucky charms, particularly around exam season.

The plethora of beliefs that surround this tiny grain is astounding. These beliefs and superstitions only highlight the social importance of fonio in our communities. Fonio is not just any grain. It has a powerful story. Whenever we cook fonio, we are preserving the planet's biodiversity while maintaining a tradition that dates back thousands of years.

Fonio facts: a summary

Fonio is the world's fastest-growing cereal. In low-rainfall regions, it can mature in 45 to 60 days and in high-rainfall areas, between two and four months. Thanks to this fast growth, fonio is considered to be a life-saving bounty or manna come "hungry season," when barns are empty and next season's harvest is not ready yet. In the Sahel countries, where irrigation is nonexistent and farmers mainly rely on a short rainfall season for agriculture, this is a real blessing.

Fonio's cultivation is for the most part manual and quite easy. Following the first rain, the fonio farmer barely loosens the soil with her hoe and simply broadcasts the seeds across the field. The average weight of seeds planted per hectare (2.47 acres) varies between 10 and 30 kilograms (22 to 66 pounds) but can sometimes go up to 50 kilograms (about 110 pounds), with harvesting yield varying from 0.2 to 0.5 metric tons per hectare.

Fonio grows into an annual plant 45 to 50 centimeters (17 to 20 inches) tall, with deep roots that are embedded in the soil. Its ability to enrich the soil helps prevent erosion, a leading cause of desertification.

There are two major cultivated species of fonio: *Digitaria exilis*, known as white fonio, and *Digitaria iburua* or black fonio, which is not actually black in color, but rather light tan. White fonio, the most commonly grown, is mainly cultivated from Senegal to Chad, while black fonio is grown in the Jos Plateau region of Nigeria and in the northern regions of Togo and Benin. There is not much of a flavor difference between white and black fonio, but black fonio comes out a little softer when cooked.

Climate

Fonio is grown in tropical climates with a long dry season and average temperatures of 24º to 32ºC (75º to 90ºF). The average rainfall is between 400 and 2000 millimeters (16 to 79 inches) per year. However, fonio can also grow in higher elevations as is done in Guinea, where it is produced in areas that are over 1000 meters (about 3281 feet) above sea level, with cooler temperatures and higher rainfall.

Soil

Fonio tolerates poor soil and is often planted on light sandy, or even stony, soils.

When grown in richer soils, fonio is grown in rotation with other crops such as rice, millet, sorghum, or groundnut.

The Journey of Fonio

IN THE FALL of 2018, my photographer, Adam Bartos, and I set out for southern Senegal to document the harvesting of fonio first-hand.

Early October usually marks the beginning of harvest season in the region of Sedhiou. Because the rainy season came later than expected this year, the harvest was delayed by a couple of weeks.

Our quest to find a field being harvested was more challenging than expected.

Driving between the crossroad known as Croisement N'diaye and the village of Djende, we passed through countless fonio fields stretching on both sides of the road, hedged by palm and cashew trees from the Casamance forest sweeping the horizon. Unlike the typical farmland with neatly lined rows of produce, fonio fields resemble wild grass covering expansive areas. This is due to the "lazy farmer's" method of cultivating fonio by simply scattering the seeds across a field.

Cultivation

Fonio cultivation begins after the first rainfalls, which used to come around June or July. In recent years, because of climate change, rainfall has been inconsistent and most fields are not yet ready for harvest in early October. Fortunately, regardless of the inconsistent weather, resilient fonio never fails to grow once it is planted.

When we finally arrived, the plants were still standing tall, but most were already beginning to bend under the weight of the ripening grains. In about another week or two, they would all be completely lodged—that is, bent over to the ground—signaling that they were ready to be harvested.

Harvesting

Sedhiou is a large rural community located near the Casamance River, with a population of approximately 45,000 people. Its residents are a mix of Mandinka, Jola, and Fulani people. It is one of Senegal's main fonio-growing regions. Traditionally, farm activities are gender based. While men are in charge of the harvest, most of the fonio processing is done by women.

Fatou Niabali lives in the village of Nyama in the region of Sedhiou. She is a teacher at the local elementary school. Like most Mandinka women of her village, Fatou is also a fonio farmer. That year, her field was one of the first ones to be ready for harvest.

Planning the harvest requires some organizational and leadership skills. First she needed to assemble the boys to cut the fonio. Coordinating a group of teenage boys from the village during school summer break was not an easy task. Their time was split between the popular *navetanes* soccer tournaments that take place during school break in all the cities, towns, and villages of Senegal, and the equally important task of dancing and singing alongside the Kankourang.

The Kankourang is a mythical creature that also appears during the rainy season (summer) to mark initiation into Mandinka society. He comes covered from head to toe in a robe made from dark red bark. It is believed that the individual who dresses in the frightening-looking outfit of Kankourang loses his ego to become a spirit. He always appears in public during initiation, when thousands of future initiates enter the sacred forest as boys and return to their families days later as adults.

The initiation is an important part of the educational process among the Mandinkas. Its teaching, based on the union of body and soul, is related to justice and social morality. The learning ritual takes place in the sacred forest and remains a secret that initiates can never reveal to noninitiates.

In addition to getting the boys ready for harvest, Fatou also had to gather the women who would accompany the teenage

Boubacar Dramé

boys in the field. Their role was to sing revitalizing songs that showcase the bravery of the fonio farmers. The singing was often done in a call-and-response manner, all in a joyful atmosphere that sometimes included rhythmic dances. The goal of these songs was to raise the boys' morale and to keep them working in rhythm, to be more productive and to better endure the arduous work of cutting fonio. (This ancient tradition was exported to the Americas during the slave trade and became plantation work songs.) Lastly, Fatou also gathered up younger boys aged 8 to 12. Their role was to collect the cut fonio into piles which would be later tied in large bundles by the older boys.

The fonio in Fatou's field were lodging like overgrown grass after a strong wind. This tendency to lodge made it difficult to harvest because it must all be done manually with the use of a *daba* (sickle). The teenage boys, each equipped with a daba, lined up across the edge of the field. They looked focused and ready to tackle the task. The women were standing behind them, also in line, but looking more relaxed and cheerful. Behind the women were the ever-playful younger boys. A whistle was blown and the work began.

The boys, bent, grabbed shafts of fonio, cut them at their base with their dabas, dropped the shafts on the field, and repeated while moving forward. The women sang and clapped and even danced. Sometimes, the teenage boys also stopped to execute a rhythmic and energizing dance move before returning to work. Behind the women, the younger boys, excited to play a part in this festive operation, neatly assembled the cut fonio into big bundles which would be later tied up with ropes made from bark of the surrounding trees.

Soon, Fatou's field was completely cleaned. Large stacks of freshly harvested fonio were piled in one end of the field, neatly tied into large bundles. The cheering women were now in charge of bringing the fonio back to the village where it would be transformed. Each woman skillfully put a bundle on her head and carried it with astonishing balance, grace, and good humor back to the village for processing.

Processing

Before being ready for consumption, fonio needs first to be separated from its inedible hull. The tiny size of the fonio grains makes this operation laborious. Even after Sanoussi Diakité, a Senegalese engineer, won the Rolex Prize in 1996 for his invention of the first fonio processing machine, much of the production work still remains manual. Harvesting is still done by hand with a scythe. Threshing is also done the old-fashioned way, on a straw mat or a tarp placed on a hard floor, by crushing the crops with bare feet to separate the straw from the grains.

Following threshing and hulling, grains are still manually washed in large hollowed calabashes filled with water.

In Casamance, most of the postharvest work is done by women. Men were traditionally in charge of harvest activities but with more men leaving villages to find work in the city, these tasks are relegated more often to women these days. Needless to say, labor requirements remain high and working hours long.

Mañima Camara lives in the village of Hainou Salam, located in the commune of Djende in Sedhiou. Hainou Salam is a peaceful and beautiful village with huts made with straw roofs and mud walls. Mañima's house is a large mud brick structure, surrounded by a bamboo fence. In her vast courtyard, large mango trees with branches full of birds' nests offer much-welcome shade during the hot and humid rainy season days, while the loud symphony of hundreds of little black and yellow birds' melodic chirping greets the visitors.

Mañima processes and sells fonio in the market to support her young children. She is reputed to have the cleanest fonio in the community and she often sells out at the market. Her husband recently passed away after a long illness. As a new widow, she wore a scarf to cover her head for a period of forty days as part of a mourning ritual.

Mañima gets her fonio directly from local farmers, particularly from Boubacar Dramé, one of Mañima's husband's best friends. The fresh fonio is first sun-dried on an elevated platform for several days, covered with a cloth to protect it from birds and inclement weather.

Boubacar's wife, Mariama, helps Mañima with the tedious fonio processing work. They placed the dried fonio harvest on a tarp directly on the floor and together, they began threshing it with their bare feet to separate the grains from the stalks. The trick was to gradually squeeze stalks of fonio between the feet. In some places, the stalks are threshed by hand with a stick.

Mañima's threshing area is always meticulously cleaned beforehand to avoid soiling the grains. The threshing floor is hard, made from a mixture of clay and earth that's been beaten to a solid and compact ground. While the leftover straw from the threshing is removed to be used for animal feed, the grains are winnowed with woven baskets or sieves, or simply by fanning them while they're on the tarp. Following the winnowing, the grains are usually saved in clay granaries, where they can be stored for years before being sold in paddy (fonio harvested but before processing, fonio in the husk) or hulled for consumption.

Since Mañima was planning to prepare a few of her fonio specialties, she needed to hull and whiten the fonio right away. This process is done with a large wooden mortar and pestle. Hers is carved out of a mango tree trunk. She put some whole, unhulled fonio in the mortar. With two pestles almost as tall as they are, Mañima and Mariama proceeded to pound the fonio grains to remove their hulls.

Pounding is a synchronized art form. Mañima and Mariama's cadenced beat turned the mortar and pestle into a musical instrument. At times, they even sang along. The range of the thumping sound varied depending on which angle the mortar was hit. The ladies were swinging and grooving.

They pounded, then winnowed the fonio several times with a fine-mesh sieve, until it was completely cleaned of its hull and white in color. Gradually, the cleaned fonio was placed in a large bowl and replaced in the mortar with fresh, uncleaned fonio for more rhythmic pounding. This laborious work barely produced between 1 and 2 kilograms (2 ¼ to 4 ½ pounds) of hulled fonio per hour of pounding.

At times, younger girls took over the pounding to allow Mañima and Mariama time to tackle other tasks, such as collecting water from the well behind the house. With it, they washed the hulled fonio several times until it was completely free of bran and of any sand that may have collected during the harvest.

Once the fonio was washed, Mañima wrapped and tied it in a clean muslin cloth that she then suspended from a pole in the ceiling of her kitchen to drain. Once the fonio was well drained, Mañima had two options: cook it immediately or sun-dry it.

Sun-drying fonio is done by spreading the grains on a tarp placed on an elevated wooden platform, located in an open sunny area of the courtyard. Once the water has completely evaporated, the dried fonio would then be stored in her granary until needed.

Cooking

To cook it, Mañima put the drained fonio in a large clay colander and steamed it over boiling water. To prevent the steam from escaping, she sealed the gap between the colander and the boiling pot by applying a paste of water and ash from the burning logs. She cooked the fonio until it was light and fluffy. At this stage, she could also sun-dry it, then package it in plastic bags to sell at the market. Today, Mañima decided to prepare a few of her favorite dishes for the whole family to enjoy with fonio: palm nut and vegetable stew, baobab leaf sauce, and lamb with peanut sauce. (For my versions of these dishes, see pages 100, 101, and 115.)

Mañima has another method of preparing fonio that doesn't require steaming.

She lights a big fire using logs placed among three large stones of approximately the same size. She sets a large cast-iron pot directly on the fire and places in it whole fonio grains that are not yet hulled. In the pot, she toasts the fonio with the husks on,

stirring frequently, until it turns dark brown and begins to pop. This technique adds a lovely smoky flavor to the fonio. It can then be pounded to remove the hulls, then pounded again into a delicious paste and afterward sweetened with honey or sugar.

The journey of fonio highlights the place of women in Mandinka society. They are a source of stability and, above all, a vital link to their family's prosperity.

Brewing

Fonio is brewed into a popular beer in some regions of West Africa, particularly in Togo, Côte d'Ivoire, and Burkina Faso. The beer is known as *tchapalo* and nicknamed *tchap*. The brewing process can be very simple: Fonio grains are soaked and germinated covered with cassava leaves, then dried, ground into flour, and diluted with water. The mash is heated over a fire, then allowed to sit at room temperature for a few days, covered with fabric or leaves, until it ferments. This artisanal brew will keep fermenting as time passes so it is usually consumed soon after it is prepared; it doesn't keep well and has a strong fermented flavor. Tchap is sold in local bars, stored in clay pots and served in a calabash that's passed around among the drinking buddies.

Tchapalo is also served during ritual ceremonies to invoke the ancestors' spirits. Locals always pour a few drops to the ground before drinking as a symbolic ritual to share with the ancestors. In the Senufo tribe, as in many West African communities, tchapalo is prepared by women who learn the process during a secret society initiation for women.

Nutrition and health

Let thy food be thy medicine and thy medicine be thy food.
—Attributed to Hippocrates

When I was a kid growing up in Senegal, food was always part of treating any illnesses. My grandmother, in fact, had a food remedy handy for almost any ailment.

For malaria, she would prepare a dense *soupou yell* (cow feet soup) with a broth of slowly simmered meat, thickened by the cartilage that melted from the feet and knuckles. Grandma would cook it in one pot along with yucca, carrots, garlic, cloves, cumin, and hot pepper. For the flu, a migraine, and even hangovers, she would serve *pepe* soup, a whole fish poached in a light broth with onions, tomatoes, Scotch bonnet pepper, and lime juice, that was somehow very soothing.

Fonio itself belongs to a category of foods that performs a dual role in our medicine. It heals the physical body, and is also believed to protect against unseen ill-intentioned djinns or bad spells. In our society, magic and sorcery are still alive and kicking. Some people in Casamance continue to grow fonio around their compounds, believing in its hidden protective properties.

Fonio Compared with Other Popular Grains

	Quick Cooking (<10 min)	Gluten Free	Low Glycemic Index (<60)	Nutritionally Dense
Fonio	●	●	●	●
Brown Rice		●		
White Rice		●		
Couscous	●			
Quinoa		●		●
Farro				●
Barley				●
Freekeh				●
Oat		●		●
Teff		●		●
Millet		●		●

Regardless of its alleged mystical properties, several studies suggest that fonio could be an important source of nutrients critical to human health.

A Nutrition Powerhouse

As today's nutrition-conscious consumers, we must look beyond trends and explore ingredients that are unfamiliar in order to enrich our diets and save our planet's biodiversity.

Fonio, Celiac Disease, and Diabetes

Fonio is gluten-free, and as such is an excellent grain for people suffering from celiac disease or any type of gluten intolerance. And unlike other refined grains, fonio doesn't cause spikes in blood sugar levels. Fonio is low on the glycemic index, which is why in Senegal and other countries in the region, it is recommended to diabetics. However, although fonio scores lower than most cereals on the glycemic index, it should still be consumed with moderation to be beneficial to diabetics. In addition, fonio's high fiber content, particularly of cellulose, helps regulate diabetes by reducing carbohydrate intake. Of course, a fonio diet for diabetics should be accompanied with

sauces or sides that are not too rich in lipids such as peanuts, and richer in vegetables like okra.

Digestion and Weight Loss

Fonio is easily digested, and metabolizes slowly. As a result, it provides a slow release of energy, allowing you to eat ample portions without feeling heavy and discomforted. This slow release helps to maintain constant energy levels throughout the day, enough to last until your next meal. Fonio is recommended as a diet against obesity, and in folk medicine, fonio is used as a remedy for stomachaches as it reduces constipation.

Researchers are just beginning to study the health benefits of fonio, and as of this book's writing, there are not yet as many in-depth studies available as there are for other popular grains. The information presented here has been researched from a few recent studies. If you are interested in learning more about the nutritional content of fonio, please refer to the bibliography on page 169.

Comparison of Nutrient Values

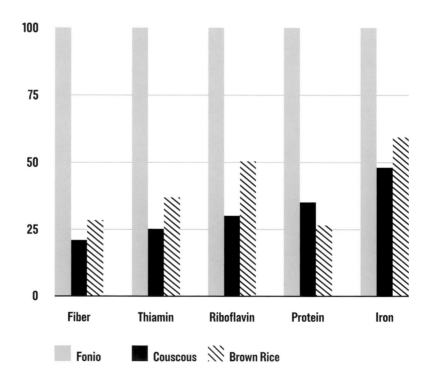

Ingredients in this book

These are common ingredients that are traditionally used with fonio, many which can be easily found in African markets or online (see page 168), though there are also substitutes in American supermarkets.

Cassava: Cassava, also known as yucca, is a root vegetable consumed in most of West and Central Africa. It has a thick, dark brown skin and crunchy white flesh. Although it originated in South America and arrived in Africa during the Columbian Exchange, today it is considered the "African potato" due to its popularity. It is starchy and is often used to prepare *fufu* (see the dumplings on page 75). In Côte d'Ivoire, cassava is fermented and grated to a couscous-like texture to make a side dish called *atieke*. In Ghana, Liberia, and Nigeria, a cassava grits dish called *gari* is very popular. In the US, cassava is mostly consumed in the form of tapioca, though it is also popular in Mexican cooking and can be found in many Mexican markets here.

Yams: Often confused with sweet potatoes, yams are also a tuber. But unlike sweet potatoes, yams have hairy skins and flesh that is white, starchy, and dry. Yams are very popular in the West African diet, particularly in their pounded form known as pounded yam or fufu.

Bitter eggplant: Bitter eggplant is also known as the bitter tomato, Ethiopian eggplant, *nakati*, or *diaxatou*. Grown mainly in Asia and Africa, it's shaped like a tomato and can be boiled, steamed, fried, or cooked in stews with meat and other vegetables.

Baobab leaf powder (lalo): A powder made from dried leaves of the baobab tree, *lalo* is used as a seasoning and a thickener in the traditional Senegalese kitchen. Because of its mucilaginous properties, lalo is used in almost all the classic millet or fonio couscous recipes in Senegalese cooking.

Fonio flour: Finely ground fonio is easy to make at home (see page 57). It can be used to make pastries and breads, or as a thickener in sauces.

Peanut flour: Made from powdered raw peanuts, peanut flour is used in Guinea and South Senegal. Also known as *noflaye* in Wolof, it has a fresher and earthier flavor than peanut butter.

Moringa powder: Moringa powder is made from dried moringa leaves. Moringa is considered a superfood because of its high protein content. It is important that the leaves be dried immediately after they are collected, otherwise they lose many of their nutritional properties. In South Senegal and Guinea, moringa leaves are used fresh in chunky sauces, often combined with palm oil and peanut flour. Because of its rich nutrient content, it is popularly called *nevedaye* in Senegal (as in "never die").

Red palm oil: Extracted from the outer flesh of the palm fruit, red palm oil is healthier than the highly processed pale-colored palm kernel oil, extracted from the fruit's seeds, that Americans are more familiar with. Red palm oil has a rich, savory flavor and high vitamin E and beta-carotene content. Because of high demand, red palm oil is often vilified for its environmental impact, mostly in the rainforests of Southeast Asia. However, the truth is that palm trees produce more oil and use less land than crops that produce other common cooking oils (olive, grapeseed, soybean, and avocado, to name a few). So replacing palm oil with these oils will have a greater negative impact on the environment. Nevertheless, we should still be mindful of the environmental impact when cooking with it and always seek sustainable palm oil. Look for palm oil products certified by the Roundtable on Sustainable Palm Oil (RSPO), such as Nutiva, or source fair-trade palm oil from smallholder producers in West and Central Africa like the Serendipalm cooperative in Ghana, many of whom already apply RSPO's principles. Palm oil is also known as dendé oil in Brazil, where it arrived from West Africa during the Atlantic Trade.

Dawadawa/Nététou: Also known as *nététou* in Senegal or *soumbala* by the Bambara, dawadawa is the Yoruba name for fermented locust beans. It has a strong, pungent flavor similar to that of Japanese natto or Chinese fermented black beans. It is used in most cuisines of West Africa as a seasoning, bringing umami depth to sauces and stews. Dawadawa can be found at African markets or on Amazon in a powdered form.

Palm nuts: Palm nuts, the fruits of the palm tree, come in large clusters that grow from the top of the tree. Traditionally, the nuts are separated with a machete. Both the oil and flesh are used. To prepare palm oil, you must first cook the nuts in boiling water until softened, then pound and strain the result to extract the oil. The flesh of palm nuts is used in countless sauces all over West Africa. My favorite dish with palm nuts is *banga*, a thick stew from Nigeria cooked with crayfish and seafood or meat.

Fish sauce: Known as *nuoc mam* in Vietnam and Senegal, it has become part of the Senegalese pantry thanks to the small Vietnamese community that arrived in Senegal in the 1950s during the First Indochina War, while Vietnam and Senegal were still under French colonial rule. (Foods like nuoc mam and

Palm nuts

Top: cassava; bottom: dried hibiscus flowers

nem—spring rolls—are now mainstream in Senegal.) Fish sauce is a good substitute for *yett*, the fermented conch that adds so much flavor to our national dish, *thiebou jenn*. Fish sauce's flavor and funky smell is practically indistinguishable from that of yett.

Tamarind paste/tamarind pulp: The uses for tamarind pulp (the flesh extracted from the tamarind pod) are diverse. You can use it to prepare a drink, or as a fruity and acidic addition to sauces or stews. Growing up in Dakar, one of my favorite snacks was the spicy and savory *niambaan*, a relish made with tamarind, salt, hot pepper powder, and fresh onion. The name of the city of Dakar originates from *dakhar*, the Wolof name for tamarind.

Black-eyed pea leaves: Leaves in general have always been a big part of the West African diet. They are nutritious and recommended for a balanced diet. Black-eyed pea or *niébé* leaves can be used in slaws or in salads or simply sautéed like spinach.

Pumpkin seeds: Known in countries of the region as *egusi*, the shelled seeds from pumpkins and other melons are ground and used to thicken stews, soups, and sauces. Ground raw peanuts can be used instead.

Dried hibiscus flowers: Sorrel, roselle, hibiscus, and *bisaap* are only a few of the names for the same little blossom. Both red and white flowers are used to make a refreshing beverage in Africa and throughout the African diaspora.

BASIC RECIPES

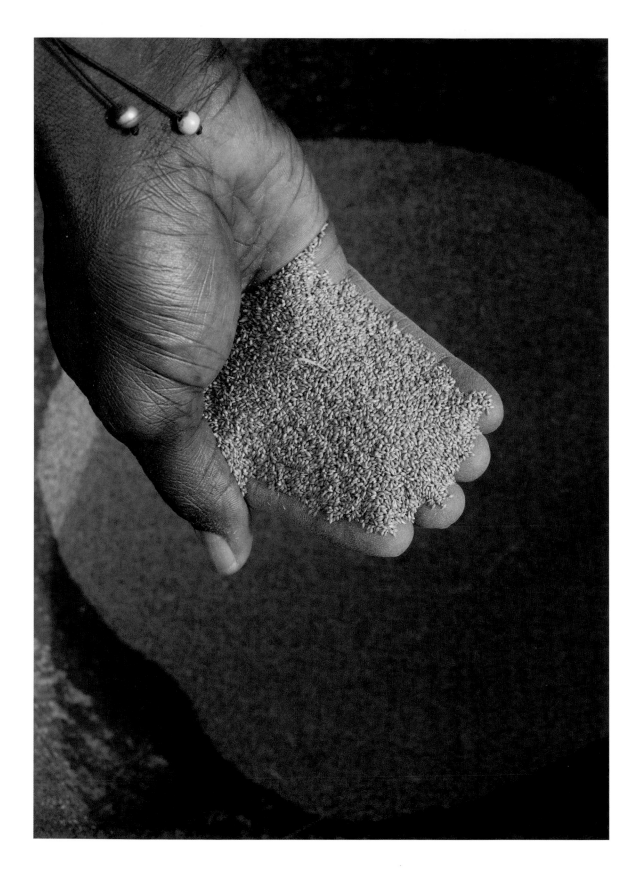

Basic Fonio

Steaming, the most common of the traditional methods of preparing fonio, is a foolproof way to avoid overcooking the grains, but cooking it on the stovetop is an easy alternative if you don't have a double boiler. Adding oil is optional but if you do, the grains will have a richer, fluffier texture and will keep separated.

Raw fonio can be stored for up to 2 years in a sealed container or resealable plastic bag at room temperature or in the refrigerator. Cooked fonio can be kept refrigerated in a covered plastic or glass container for 2 or 3 days.

INGREDIENTS

- 1 cup raw fonio, rinsed and drained well
- 1 teaspoon salt
- 1 tablespoon vegetable, peanut, or olive oil
- 1 teaspoon baobab leaf powder (lalo) mixed with ¼ cup water, or 2 tablespoons finely chopped okra
- 3½ cups water plus ½ cup for sprinkling

MAKES 3 TO 4 CUPS

Traditional Steamer Method One

Lalo, a powder made with dried baobab leaves, is used as a seasoning and a thickener in Senegal, although here you can also use finely chopped okra as a substitute.

PREPARATION

1. Line the perforated steamer top of a double boiler with cheese-cloth. Fill the bottom with 3 cups water and bring to a simmer.

2. Place the fonio in the top of the double boiler, cover, and steam for about 15 minutes, until the fonio is light and fluffy.

3. Remove from heat. Fold in the oil and the baobab powder mixture or the okra. Fluff the fonio with a fork and mix in the salt.

4. Sprinkle the fonio evenly with the remaining 1/2 cup water, cover, and return to the heat for another 10 minutes or until the fonio grains are tender and fluffy. Fluff again with a fork and serve.

Traditional Steamer Method Two

INGREDIENTS

1   cup raw fonio, rinsed and drained well

3 ½ (about) cups water

1   teaspoon salt

1   tablespoon peanut, vegetable, or olive oil (optional)

MAKES 3 TO 4 CUPS

PREPARATION

1. Line a steamer basket with cheesecloth and place it in a large saucepan. Pour in about 3 cups water to fill the pan up but not touching the bottom of the basket. Bring the water to a simmer.

2. Place the fonio in the basket, cover, and steam for about 15 minutes, until the fonio is light and fluffy.

3. Remove from the heat and fluff with a fork. Mix the salt with the remaining 1/2 cup water and sprinkle evenly over the fonio. Cover, return to the heat, and steam until the grains are tender, another 8 to 10 minutes.

4. Fluff again with a fork. Mix in the oil (if using). Serve.

Stovetop Method

INGREDIENTS

2   cups water

1   teaspoon salt

1   cup raw fonio, rinsed and drained well

1   tablespoon peanut, vegetable, or olive oil (optional)

MAKES 3 TO 4 CUPS

PREPARATION

1. Combine the water and salt in a saucepan and bring to a boil. Add the fonio and stir once. Reduce the heat to a simmer and cover tightly. Cook for about 5 minutes, until the water is absorbed.

2. Turn off the heat and keep the pot covered for another 2 minutes. Fluff with a fork. Mix in the oil (if using), and serve.

Microwave Method

INGREDIENTS

1   cup raw fonio, rinsed and
    drained well

2   cups water

1   teaspoon salt

MAKES 3 TO 4 CUPS

PREPARATION

1. Place the fonio in a large microwave-safe bowl and add the water and salt.

2. Cover tightly with plastic wrap and microwave on high for 6 to 8 minutes, until the water is absorbed and the fonio is tender.

3. Uncover carefully, fluff with a fork, and serve.

Fonio Flour

INGREDIENTS

2   cups raw fonio

SPECIAL EQUIPMENT
High-powered blender
such as a Vitamix, or electric
spice grinder
Fine-mesh sieve

MAKES 3 CUPS

Preparing fonio flour is quite easy and can be done with a blender or a spice grinder at home. Traditionally, we use a mortar and pestle that takes much longer, but this method has the advantage of not generating heat from the blade of a blender or spice grinder.

Freshly ground fonio flour should be kept in an airtight container in a cool, dark area; stored properly, it should last for about 2 months. If you make bulk amounts, storing it in the refrigerator or freezer can help fonio flour last for years.

PREPARATION

1. Put the fonio in the blender and make sure the lid is on tightly. Turn on the blender to the highest setting. Grind for about 30 seconds. Stop the blender and let the fonio settle. Remove the lid and stir with a rubber spatula. Place the lid back on and grind until it turns into flour.

2. Sift the flour through a fine-mesh sieve. Store in an airtight container or heavy-duty resealable plastic bag at room temperature, in a cool, dark area, or in the refrigerator or freezer; it will last longest if refrigerated or frozen.

STARTERS & SIDES

Fonio Croquettes Stuffed with Shiitake Rof & Tamarind Sauce

This recipe was inspired by *thiebou jenn*, the national dish of Senegal. Thiebou jenn is a rice, fish, and vegetable dish cooked in a tomato broth and seasoned with fermented flavors. Here, the rice is replaced with fonio. The croquette shape is reminiscent of the balls of rice formed when we eat thiebou jenn with our hands. The shiitake mushroom filling is seasoned with *rof*, the same spicy Scotch bonnet, garlic, and parsley mixture used to stuff the fish in thiebou jenn. The sweet acidity of the tamarind sauce balances and accentuates the earthiness and spiciness of the mushroom mixture.

INGREDIENTS

Kosher salt

½ pound cassava (yucca), peeled and cut into 2-inch chunks

1 cups cooked fonio

1 tablespoon vegetable oil, plus more for greasing the baking sheet

1 tablespoon tomato paste

½ cup vegetable broth, plus more if needed

1 teaspoon freshly ground black pepper

½ cup Shiitake Rof (recipe follows)

Tamarind Sauce (page 62), for serving

MAKES 10 TO 15 CROQUETTES

PREPARATION

1. Bring a large pot of salted water to a boil. Add the cassava and cook for about 10 minutes, until very soft and easily pierced with a fork. Drain the cassava and place it in a large bowl. Let cool for a few minutes. Remove and discard the hard, stringy core. Mash the cassava well. Add the fonio and combine thoroughly.

2. Preheat oven to 375°F. Lightly oil a rimmed baking sheet.

3. In a small saucepan, heat the oil over medium heat. Add the tomato paste and reduce the heat to low. Cook, stirring frequently, until the paste is dark red. If necessary, add a little water or vegetable broth from time to time to avoid scorching.

4. Add the broth and stir well to combine. Bring to a boil, then reduce the heat and simmer for 15 to 20 minutes, until thick enough to coat the back of a spoon. Season with the pepper. Remove from the heat and gradually stir into the cassava-fonio mixture until completely moistened and thick enough to compact into balls, but not too wet or dry to fall apart. Let the dough cool.

5. Divide the dough into 10 to 15 portions. Using your hands, shape each portion into a little oval croquette. Make an indentation in the center of each with your thumb and stuff with a generous pinch of the shiitake rof mixture. Carefully enclose the filling and rework the dough into a smooth oval croquette. Place on the prepared baking sheet.

6. Bake the croquettes for 10 to 15 minutes, until lightly brown and crisp. Serve hot with tamarind sauce.

Shiitake Rof

INGREDIENTS

1 tablespoon vegetable oil

1 cup shiitake mushroom caps, finely chopped

3 garlic cloves

1 bunch parsley, coarsely chopped

1 white onion, coarsely chopped

3 scallions, chopped

1 vegetable bouillon cube (optional) or 1 teaspoon salt

1 tablespoon red chile flakes

1 tablespoon freshly ground black pepper

SPECIAL EQUIPMENT
Food processor or mortar and pestle

MAKES ABOUT 2 CUPS

You can also use this as a sauce by simply adding a few tablespoons of good olive oil. I use it as a dipping sauce or drizzle it over grilled meat, fish, or vegetables. This will keep for 2 or 3 days in an airtight container.

PREPARATION

1. Heat the oil in a skillet over medium heat. Add the mushrooms and cook, stirring occasionally, until softened and aromatic. Transfer to a bowl and let cool slightly.

2. Purée the garlic, parsley, onion, scallions, bouillon cube (if using), chile flakes, and pepper in a food processor, or pound to a purée in a mortar with a pestle. Add to the mushrooms and stir well.

Tamarind Sauce

INGREDIENTS

6 ounces tamarind pulp with seeds

½ (about) cup boiling water

¾ cup honey

¼ cup fish sauce

2 garlic cloves, minced

1 Scotch bonnet pepper or habanero chile, stemmed, seeded, and minced

MAKES ABOUT 1½ CUPS

This sauce will keep in an airtight container in the refrigerator for up to one week. It makes a great marinade and glaze as well; use it in the Tamarind Roast Chicken on page 106.

PREPARATION

1. In a small bowl, cover the tamarind with the boiling water and let stand for 10 minutes to soften.

2. Using your fingers, break the tamarind apart, then let stand for another 5 minutes. Place a fine-mesh sieve over a bowl and pour in the tamarind pulp, seeds, and water. Using a rubber spatula or spoon, press the tamarind pulp through the sieve; discard the seeds and fibers. Add the honey, fish sauce, garlic, and Scotch bonnet to the strained tamarind pulp and stir to a smooth sauce.

Fonio Fritters (Fini Ngomi)

INGREDIENTS

Kosher salt

1 cup 2-inch chunks peeled sweet potato or ripe plantain

1 cup raw fonio, rinsed and drained well

4 cups water

1 cup fonio flour

1½ cups sugar

1 teaspoon instant yeast

Vegetable oil, for frying

MAKES ABOUT 10 FRITTERS

These street food fritters originate in Mali, particularly in the Sikasso, Senoufo, Minianka, and Bamanan regions. They can be addictive. Start the preparation a day before, as the dough needs to sit for at least 6 hours at room temperature for good fermentation.

These are delicious on their own, but can also be served with powdered sugar or a jam if you wish.

PREPARATION

1. Bring a large pot of salted water to a boil. Add the sweet potato and cook for about 10 minutes, until very soft and easily pierced with a fork. Drain the sweet potato and place it in a large bowl. Let cool for a few minutes. Remove and discard any strings and mash the sweet potato well.

2. In a pot over medium heat, prepare a thin porridge by stirring together the fonio and water for about 5 minutes.

3. Add the fonio porridge and fonio flour to the sweet potato. Mix well. Stir in the sugar and yeast. Cover loosely with cheesecloth and let the dough sit at room temperature for about 6 hours, or overnight, to ferment. It will have fermented enough when the dough starts bubbling and there is a light yeasty or beer-like smell.

4. When you're ready to cook the fritters, heat about 2 inches of oil in a skillet over medium-high heat. Line a plate with paper towels.

5. Give the dough a stir to recombine it, if necessary. Test the heat of the oil by dropping in a small bit of the dough; the oil is hot enough when the dough sizzles on contact. Using an ice cream scoop, scoop out portions of dough and drop them in the oil. Fry the fritters in batches, without crowding the pan, for 3 to 4 minutes on each side, until golden brown. Remove with a perforated spoon and drain briefly on the paper towels. Serve hot.

Collard Greens & Pumpkin Seed Sauce

INGREDIENTS

Kosher salt

1   bunch collard greens, stemmed and cut crosswise into 1-inch ribbons (2 packed cups)

2   tablespoons vegetable oil

1   onion, finely chopped

1   garlic clove, minced

2   tablespoons tomato paste

2   cups chopped peeled tomatoes (canned are fine)

1   bay leaf

2   cups vegetable stock or water

1½   cups ground pumpkin seeds (egusi) or ground raw peanuts

1   teaspoon salt

Pinch of freshly ground black pepper

Pinch of cayenne pepper (optional)

MAKES ABOUT 2 CUPS

PREPARATION

1. Bring a large pot of salted water to a boil. Add the collard greens and cook for about 5 minutes, until they have wilted but are still bright green. Drain in a colander and run under cold water to stop the cooking. Squeeze out excess water. Finely chop the collard greens and set them aside.

2. In a large pot, heat the oil over medium heat. Add the onion. Stir and cook for about 5 minutes, until the onions are softened but not brown. Add the garlic and stir for 1 to 2 minutes. Stir in the tomato paste and reduce the heat to low. Cook for 8 to 10 minutes, stirring frequently to avoid scorching, until well blended and fragrant. Stir in the chopped tomatoes and bay leaf. Bring to a boil, then reduce the heat to a simmer. Cook slowly for another 5 minutes.

3. Add the vegetable stock. Bring back to a boil and reduce to a simmer again. Cook for another 10 minutes, until the sauce is slightly thickened. Add the pumpkin seeds. Simmer for about 5 minutes, stirring frequently. Add the collard greens, salt, black pepper, and cayenne (if using). Stir well and simmer for another 10 minutes, until the tomatoes are completely broken down and the collard greens are soft.

4. Adjust the seasoning with salt and pepper if needed. Serve with fonio dumplings, plain fonio, or rice.

Fonio with Black Sesame Seeds

INGREDIENTS

¼ cup black sesame seeds

2 cups water

1 cup raw fonio, rinsed and drained well

¼ teaspoon salt

MAKES 3 TO 4 CUPS

PREPARATION

1. Heat a small skillet over low heat. Toast the sesame seeds until fragrant, about 1 minute. Remove from the heat.

2. Bring the water to a boil in a small saucepan over high heat. Stir in the sesame seeds, fonio, and salt. Bring back to a boil. Reduce the heat to low. Cover and simmer until the water has been absorbed, about 5 minutes. Fluff the fonio with a fork and serve.

Fonio Steamed with Okra (Foyo)

INGREDIENTS

2 cups raw fonio, rinsed and drained well

5 cups water

Salt

2 cups chopped or thinly sliced okra

MAKES 5 TO 6 CUPS

The classic and traditional way of preparing fonio is to steam it in a *couscoussière*, a two-part pot designed for cooking couscous. Steaming may seem intimidating but it's really easy. It can even be done without a couscoussière. All you need is a covered pot large enough to fit a colander.

This method of preparing fonio is practiced in Mali, Guinea, and Burkina Faso, where fonio with okra is traditionally served with meat or fish in a tomato or peanut sauce. The versatility of this dish makes it a perfect side dish for any vegan, meat, or fish recipe.

PREPARATION

1. Line the perforated steamer top of a double boiler or a large colander with cheesecloth. Fill the bottom of the double boiler with 4 cups of the water, or place the colander in a large pot and pour in the water until it barely touches the bottom of the colander. Bring the water to a simmer.

2. Place the fonio in the double-boiler or colander. Cover the pot tightly and steam for about 10 minutes, until the fonio is light and fluffy but there's still some resistance in the bite (al dente).

3. Stir in salt to taste. Evenly sprinkle the fonio with the remaining 1 cup water and stir. Cover and steam again for another 5 minutes, until soft to the bite.

4. Fold in the okra. Cover and steam for a third time for about 15 minutes, until the okra is soft. Stir and fluff with a fork. Serve hot or at room temperature.

Jollof Fonio

Many West African nations, particularly Nigeria, Ghana, and Senegal, have an ongoing fight over who makes the best *jollof* rice. If you make *jollof* with fonio instead, it is just as flavorful and even more nutritious.

INGREDIENTS

2	tablespoons vegetable oil
2	tablespoons finely chopped onion
2	tablespoons tomato paste
1	cup vegetable broth
1	teaspoon salt, plus more if needed
½	teaspoon freshly ground black pepper
4	cups cooked fonio

SERVES 4

PREPARATION

1. Heat the oil in a saucepan over medium heat. Add the onions and tomato paste and reduce the heat to low. Stir gently with a wooden spoon for about 5 minutes, until the paste is dark red but not burnt. If necessary, add a little water or some of the vegetable broth to avoid scorching.

2. Stir in the vegetable broth and season with the salt and pepper. Bring to a boil, reduce the heat, and simmer until the oil rises to the surface, another 15 to 20 minutes.

3. Fold in the cooked fonio until well combined. Adjust the seasoning with salt and pepper and serve hot.

Fonio Balls with Black-Eyed Pea Leaves

Edible leaves are never wasted in West African cooking. This is a healthy snack with black eyed pea leaves, but pretty much any leafy greens can be substituted. You can serve these as a first course or a side.

INGREDIENTS

4   cups loosely packed black-eyed pea leaves or spinach

1   teaspoon baking soda

1   cup raw fonio, rinsed and drained well

2   cups peanut flour or unsweetened smooth peanut butter

1   teaspoon salt

    Red palm oil or olive oil and cayenne pepper, for drizzling (optional)

SPECIAL EQUIPMENT
Mortar and pestle or food processor

MAKES 8 TO 10 BALLS

PREPARATION

1. Using a mortar and pestle or food processor, process the leaves until they form a paste or are very finely chopped. Transfer to a large bowl and mix in the baking soda, fonio, peanut flour, and salt.

2. Using your hands (wet them lightly will prevent sticking), shape the dough into portions the size and shape of golf balls.

3. Using a double boiler with a perforated steamer top or a large pot and steamer basket, steam the fonio balls until firm, about 30 minutes. (It is not necessary to line the steamer.)

4. Serve hot with a drizzle of palm oil or a mix of olive oil and cayenne (if using).

Djouka Fonio

This popular side dish in Mali and Burkina Faso can also be eaten as a snack. *Djouka* is typically served with Chicken Yassa (page 109), or with fish, meat, or vegetables and a tomato or onion sauce.

INGREDIENTS

- 2 cups raw fonio, rinsed and drained well
- 5 cups water
- 1 ½ cups peanut flour or unsweetened smooth peanut butter
- 1 teaspoon salt
- 2 garlic cloves, minced
- 1 pound okra pods, trimmed and chopped (optional)

SERVES 6

PREPARATION

1. Line the perforated steamer top of a double boiler with cheesecloth and steam the fonio for 10 minutes over 4 cups of the water, until light and fluffy but still al dente.

2. Sprinkle the remaining 1 cup water evenly over the fonio and slowly fold to incorporate it before steaming a second time for 5 minutes.

3. Fold in the peanut flour, salt, and garlic. Steam a third time for 10 minutes, until soft and the peanut flavor is incorporated.

4. If using the okra, in a blender or food processor, process until it is a purée. Fold the okra into the fonio and cook for another 5 minutes.

5. Serve hot.

Fonio & Smoked Shrimp Powder Beignets

These beignets are inspired by street food from Benin. Smoked shrimp powder imparts a unique umami taste, and can be found in many West African cuisines. You can buy smoked shrimp powder from African online retailers, or blend your own from smoked shrimp available from Amazon and Asian grocery stores. You can also substitute ground dried shrimp combined with a teaspoon of smoked paprika for the smoked shrimp powder.

INGREDIENTS

- 6 cups fonio flour
- 1 tablespoon vegetable oil, plus more for frying
- 1 cup smoked shrimp powder
- 4 onions, 2 grated and 2 thinly sliced
- 1½ teaspoons finely chopped ginger
- 1 Scotch bonnet pepper, seeded and minced (optional)
- 1½ teaspoons salt, plus more if needed
- ¼ teaspoon freshly ground black pepper

MAKES ABOUT
25 SMALL BEIGNETS

PREPARATION

1. Put the fonio flour in a large bowl. Add 1 tablespoon oil and mix well. Add the shrimp powder and stir to combine. Stir in the onions. Add the ginger, Scotch bonnet (if using), and the salt and black pepper and mix until well blended.

2. Pour about 2 inches of oil into a skillet or deep pot and turn on the heat to medium-high. Line a platter with paper towels. Test the heat by dropping in a small bit of dough; the oil is hot enough when the dough sizzles on contact.

3. Working in batches, use your hands, a spoon, or a small ice cream scoop to shape the dough into golf ball-sized beignets and gently add them into the hot oil. Fry for 2 to 3 minutes, turning the beignets as necessary, until golden on all sides and cooked through (cut one open to check). Remove with a perforated spoon and drain briefly on the paper towels. Serve hot.

Fonio & Cassava Dumplings (Tô Fini)

INGREDIENTS

Kosher salt

1 pound cassava (yucca), peeled and cut into 2-inch chunks

2½ quarts water

4 cups raw fonio, rinsed and drained well

1 tablespoon lemon or tamarind juice (optional)

1 tablespoon red palm oil (optional)

Collard Greens & Pumpkin Seed Sauce (recipe follows) or Mafé Sauce (page 115), for serving

MAKES ABOUT 16
LARGE DUMPLINGS

Tô is the quintessential African dumpling, very large in size. Called many different names—*fufu* in Nigeria and Congo, *futu* in Côte d'Ivoire, *tô* in Mali and Guinea, *nshima* in Zambia, *sadza* in Zimbabwe, *pap* in South Africa, and *ugali* in Kenya—it is generally prepared by pounding cooked tubers or flour. In Mali, fonio dumplings are eaten with a simple tomato sauce, okra and red palm sauce, peanut sauce, or leaf-vegetable sauce.

I sometimes add a little red palm oil to the dumpling dough, which would give them an orange hue and a velvety texture, as Ivoirians do with plantain dumplings.

PREPARATION

1. Bring a large pot of salted water to a boil. Add the cassava and cook for about 10 minutes, until very soft and easily pierced with a fork. Drain the cassava and place it in a bowl. Let cool for a few minutes. Remove and discard the hard, stringy core. Mash the cassava well.

2. Bring 2 1/2 quarts water to a boil in a large saucepan over high heat. Stir in the fonio. Cook, stirring so it does not stick, until it becomes a thick paste, about 15 minutes. Add the lemon juice (if using).

3. Gradually stir in the mashed cassava and red palm oil (if using) to obtain a dough-like consistency. Lower the heat to medium-low and continue cooking, stirring vigorously, until it becomes a thick, homogeneous paste, about another 15 minutes. Cover the pot and cook over low heat for 5 minutes more, until it becomes a smoother paste.

4. Remove from the heat and let the dough cool in the pot until it is cool enough to handle, but is still warm. Using your hands, shape into balls the size of a fist or larger. Serve immediately with collard greens sauce or mafé (peanut) sauce.

Spring Vegetable Fonio Pilaf

INGREDIENTS

2 tablespoons peanut or vegetable oil

1 shallot, thinly sliced

1 garlic clove, minced

1 large carrot, diced

½ cup vegetable or chicken broth

¼ cup fresh or frozen green peas

¼ cup fresh or frozen corn kernels

2 cups cooked fonio

2 scallions, thinly sliced

Salt and freshly ground black pepper

SERVES 4

Spring vegetables add freshness and color to fonio in this easy side dish.

PREPARATION

1. Heat the oil in a saucepan over medium-high heat. Add the shallot and cook until soft but not brown, about 1 minute. Add the garlic and carrots and cook for another 3 minutes, until the garlic is fragrant. Add the broth and simmer, covered, until the carrots are tender, about 10 minutes.

2. Add the peas and corn and cook for about 1 minute. Fold in the fonio and scallions and season with salt and pepper to taste. Serve hot or at room temperature.

Fonio, Yam & Shrimp Cakes with Harissa-Yogurt Sauce

INGREDIENTS

1	cup grated peeled yam (about ½ pound yams; not sweet potatoes)
1	tablespoon salt
1½	cups cooked fonio
3	tablespoons fonio flour
12	raw shrimp, peeled, deveined, and finely chopped (about 1 cup)
3	large eggs
1	small red onion, finely chopped
2	garlic cloves, chopped
½	jalapeño chile, seeded and minced
	Pinch of cayenne pepper
1	teaspoon fine sea salt
¼	teaspoon freshly ground black pepper
1	cup plain Greek yogurt
	Juice of 1 lime
2	tablespoons harissa
½	cup olive oil, plus more if needed

MAKES 10 CAKES AND ABOUT 1 CUP SAUCE

Harissa is a Tunisian hot pepper paste that adds a wonderful smoky flavor. The yogurt balances the heat and adds creaminess to the sauce. Serve these cakes with just the sauce, or add a green salad for a light meal.

PREPARATION

1. In a bowl, combine the yam with the salt and mix well. Let it sit for about 1 hour to allow the salt to draw excess water from the yam. Drain and squeeze the yam to remove as much water as possible.

2. In a large bowl, fold together the yam, fonio, fonio flour, shrimp, eggs, onion, garlic, jalapeño, cayenne, sea salt, and pepper until well combined. Shape into 10 or more cakes with about a 3-inch diameter.

3. In a small bowl, mix together the yogurt, lime juice, and harissa. Refrigerate until you're ready to serve.

4. Heat the oil in a heavy-bottomed skillet over medium heat. Line a plate with paper towels. Without crowding the pan, cook the cakes in the oil for 5 to 7 minutes on the first side, until crisp and golden. Turn and cook until the other side is browned, 3 to 5 minutes. Transfer the finished patties to the paper towels.

5. Add more oil as needed and continue until all the cakes are cooked. Serve the cakes with the harissa-yogurt sauce.

Fonio Crackers with Roasted Pepper & Cashew Dip

INGREDIENTS

¼ cup cooked fonio

½ cup chickpea flour or all-purpose flour

1¼ teaspoons fine sea salt

2 teaspoons ground cumin

6 tablespoons cold water, plus more if needed

2 tablespoons olive oil, plus more for the baking sheet

2 tablespoons cumin or anise seeds (optional)

Roasted Pepper & Cashew Dip (recipe follows), for serving

MAKES ABOUT 50 CRACKERS

These crackers can be prepared ahead of time and will keep in a tightly closed jar for 2 weeks. For extra flavor and texture, sprinkle the dough with cumin or anise seeds right before baking. The dipping sauce is also easy to prepare and can be ready in the refrigerator for an emergency healthy snack or to entertain your guests.

PREPARATION

1. Preheat the oven to 350°F. Line a full-size baking sheet or two half sheets with parchment paper.

2. Mix the fonio, chickpea flour, salt, and ground cumin. Combine the water with 2 tablespoons oil. Add the water and oil to the fonio mixture and mix well until just combined. If the mixture is too dry, add up to another 2 tablespoons water. Do not overmix, or the crackers will be tough.

3. Brush the parchment paper with oil, then spread the cracker batter very thinly over the paper in strips about 4 inches wide. Press it down with the spoon to make sure the layer of batter is very thin and spread evenly. If you wish, top the batter with cumin or anise seeds.

4. Bake for about 15 minutes, until firm and very lightly colored. Carefully flip over the strips and bake for another 10 to 15 minutes, until crisp and golden.

5. Remove the baking sheet from the oven and place it on a wire rack for the crackers to cool completely. Break the strips into smaller pieces. Store in an airtight container for up to 2 weeks.

Roasted Pepper & Cashew Dip

INGREDIENTS

2	large red bell peppers, roasted, peeled, and seeded
1	garlic clove, smashed and peeled
1	cup roasted cashew nuts
¼	cup tomato purée
2	tablespoons chopped fresh flat-leaf parsley
2	tablespoons wine vinegar
1	teaspoon smoked paprika
½	Scotch bonnet pepper, stemmed and seeded
½	cup extra virgin olive oil
	Fine sea salt and freshly ground black pepper

MAKES ABOUT 1 CUP

This can be stored in a covered container in the refrigerator for 2 to 3 days.

PREPARATION

1. Pulse the roasted peppers, garlic, cashews, tomato purée, parsley, vinegar, paprika, and Scotch bonnet in a food processor until very finely chopped. With the motor running, slowly add the oil and process until a smooth paste forms. Season with salt and pepper to taste.

Curried Butternut Squash Soup with Kale

INGREDIENTS

Kosher salt

1 cup peeled and diced butternut squash

2 ½ tablespoons olive oil

2 ½ cups coarsely chopped portobello mushrooms

1 onion, thinly sliced (about 1 cup)

1 baking potato, peeled and diced (about 1 cup)

1 tablespoon kosher salt, plus more if needed

1 teaspoon freshly ground black pepper

1 tablespoon red curry powder

Pinch of red chile flakes

1 quart vegetable broth

1 bunch kale, stemmed and cut crosswise into 1-inch ribbons (about 4 cups)

2 tablespoons lemon juice

1 cup cooked fonio

¼ cup Fonio Crisps (recipe follows)

½ cup chopped fresh cilantro

SERVES 4

This soup is one of my all-time favorites. It's simple, beautiful, and full of flavor. It also happens to be vegan. The optional fonio crisps add a lovely texture.

PREPARATION

1. Make an ice bath by filling a large bowl with ice and cold water. Bring a large pot of salted water to a boil. Blanch the diced butternut squash for about 3 minutes, until just soft but still mostly firm. Using a perforated spoon or sieve, remove the squash from the water and plunge into the ice bath to quickly stop the cooking. When it's cool, drain the squash and set aside.

2. Heat 1 tablespoon of the oil in a large pot over medium-high heat until shimmering. Add the mushroom, onions, and potatoes and season with salt and pepper. Cook, stirring, until the mushrooms and onions are softened, about 2 minutes. Add the curry powder and chile flakes and cook, stirring, until fragrant, about 30 seconds.

3. Add the broth, adjust the heat to maintain an active boil, and cook for about 10 minutes, until the potatoes are cooked through. Add the kale and stir until it has wilted, about 2 minutes more. Stir in the lemon juice and season with salt and pepper. Let cool slightly.

4. Working in batches if necessary, transfer the soup to a blender and blend until smooth. Strain, if desired. Return to the pot and keep warm.

5. To serve, divide the cooked fonio among the four bowls. Add the butternut squash, saving a few tablespoons for garnish. Pour the soup into the bowls and top with the reserved butternut squash, fonio crisps, and cilantro.

Fonio Crisps

INGREDIENTS

1 tablespoon coconut oil, melted, or red palm oil for red crisps, plus more for the baking sheet

2 cups cooked fonio

MAKES 2 CUPS

These fun and crunchy little fonio crisps are great to sprinkle on salads, soups, or anywhere really to bring a pleasing texture to your food. They will keep in an airtight container at room temperature for up to 1 week.

PREPARATION

1. Preheat the oven to 350° F. Lightly oil a baking sheet.

2. Stir the oil into the fonio until evenly distributed. Spread the fonio on the baking sheet in a thin, even layer. Bake for 30 minutes or until golden brown, stirring every 10 minutes to make sure it cooks evenly and doesn't scorch. Let cool completely. Transfer to an airtight container.

Toasted Fonio & Coconut Balls

INGREDIENTS

2 cups raw fonio

2 cups unsweetened shredded coconut

½ cup honey, or to taste

MAKES 6 TO 8 BALLS

This recipe was inspired by my trip to Sedhiou in South Senegal. Mañima Camara (see page 39) prepared these fonio balls by simply toasting raw fonio and pounding it into a paste. She sweetened them with honey for the perfect snack.

PREPARATION

1. Place the fonio in a skillet over high heat. Toast and stir until golden brown and fragrant, about 5 minutes. Transfer to a bowl to cool.

2. In a small skillet, toast 2 tablespoons of the shredded coconut until golden. Transfer to a plate and set aside.

3. Combine the fonio and the remaining coconut and honey in a blender. Blend on high speed until it becomes a paste.

4. Using wet hands, shape the paste into balls the size of a golf ball. Roll them in the toasted coconut to cover. Refrigerate or serve at room temperature.

Crispy Fonio Crêpes

INGREDIENTS

1 cup raw fonio, rinsed and drained

1 cup water

1 tablespoon nutritional yeast (optional)

¼ teaspoon fine sea salt

2 (about) tablespoons olive oil

2 (about) cups filling of your choice (optional)

SPECIAL EQUIPMENT
Cast-iron griddle or nonstick skillet

SERVES 4

This recipe is inspired by Indian *dosas.* I love those savory crêpes and have discovered that fermented fonio makes crispy *dosas.* Fillings can vary from sweet potatoes in peanut sauce to chutney to simply sautéed vegetables. They are great when filled with diced leftovers of Fonio, Grilled Lamb Chops & Asparagus with Mafé Sauce (page 115).

The fonio will need to soak for up to 24 hours to ferment, so plan one day ahead if you would like the crêpes for breakfast. Nutritional yeast is optional, but adds protein, vitamins, and antioxidants to these crêpes.

PREPARATION

1. Soak the fonio at room temperature in the water, loosely covered with a lid or with cheesecloth, for up to 24 hours to ferment. The fonio is fermented when it bubbles slightly and there's a faint smell like yeast or beer.

2. Drain the soaked fonio, saving the water. Blend the fonio with about half of the soaking water until creamy and fine. Add the nutritional yeast (if using), and the salt and blend again. The batter should have the consistency of pancake batter. Add more of the water if needed to get the desired consistency.

3. Heat a griddle or nonstick skillet over high heat. Brush with 2 teaspoons of the oil. Lower the heat to medium-high. Immediately ladle 1/4 cup of the batter on the middle of the griddle or pan. Spread with the bottom of the ladle or by swirling the pan in a circular fashion make a round crêpe. If using a griddle, ladle and spread as many crêpes as will fit. Let the crêpes cook for 3 to 4 minutes, until the bottom turns golden brown and crisp. Do not flip. Carefully transfer the crêpes to a serving plate (it is okay to stack them). Finish making all the crêpes in this same way. Cover to keep warm.

4. If you like, top each crêpe with a few spoonfuls of filling and fold it in half to serve.

Fonio, Cassava & Moringa Gnocchi with Red Palm Oil–Tomato Sauce

INGREDIENTS

Kosher salt

2   pounds cassava (yucca), peeled and cut into 2-inch chunks

¾   cup fonio flour, plus more as needed for rolling

1   cup moringa powder, or 2 cups tightly packed fresh moringa, finely chopped

2   large eggs

¼   cup red palm oil or olive oil

2   tablespoons chopped onion

2   cups chopped tomatoes

1   tablespoon dawadawa or 1 tablespoon fish sauce

1   teaspoon salt, plus more if needed

Freshly cracked black pepper

SPECIAL EQUIPMENT
Ricer or food mill fitted with the finest disk

SERVES 4 TO 6

Moringa is a tree nicknamed *nevedaye* in Senegal, as in "never die." It is also called the "tree of life" because of its wealth of nutritional properties. Many parts of the tree are edible, but in West Africa we love the leaves, which are the most nutritious part of the plant. They are rich in vitamins B, C, and A as well as in beta-carotene and protein. We traditionally use moringa when cooking leafy stews.

This is a take on Italian gnocchi with African flavors. The velvety texture of palm oil pairs well with the fermented *dawadawa* (locust beans used as seasoning across West Africa.)

PREPARATION

1. Bring a large pot of salted water to a boil. Add the cassava and cook for about 10 minutes, until very soft and easily pierced with a fork. Drain the cassava in a colander. Let cool for a few minutes. Remove and discard the hard, stringy core.

2. Scoop the boiled cassava into a ricer or food mill fitted with the finest disk, and mill the yucca flesh onto a clean work surface, spreading it into an even layer. Allow the steam to escape for a few minutes.

3. Scoop 1/2 cup of the fonio flour into a fine-mesh sieve and dust the flour all over the cassava. Sprinkle with the moringa.

4. Transfer the cassava-moringa mixture to a blender. Add the eggs and pulse repeatedly for about 1 minute, to cut the flour, moringa, and egg into the cassava.

5. Put the dough in a bowl and pat into a loose ball. Press the ball flat with the palms of your hands, then fold in half and press down again.

6. Scoop the remaining 1/4 cup fonio flour into the sieve and dust some over dough. Continue to gently fold and press just until it the dough comes together. (Simply fold and press—this is different from kneading bread.) Dust the fonio dough all over with flour and gently form into a log about 1 by 20 inches.

7. Clean the work surface well and dust with more flour. Dust a baking sheet with flour. Using a sharp knife, slice off a roughly 2-inch-long portion of dough. Roll it into a long rope about 1/2 inch thick; do not press hard as you roll, and dust as necessary with flour to prevent sticking. Cut the rope into 1-inch portions, trimming off uneven ends as necessary. Transfer the gnocchi to the baking sheet. Repeat with the remaining dough.

8. Bring a large pot of salted water to a boil.

9. While the water is heating, heat the oil in a large skillet over medium-high heat. Add the onions and fry, stirring occasionally,

until very soft, about 3 minutes. Add the tomatoes and simmer for 10 to 15 minutes, until the oil separates out. Add the dawadawa (if using), and stir to incorporate. Add salt and pepper to taste. Cook for another 5 minutes, until slightly reduced and thick enough to coat a spoon. Cover and keep warm over low heat.

10. Working in batches if necessary, add the gnocchi to the boiling water and gently stir once to prevent sticking. When gnocchi begin to float to the surface, 3 to 5 minutes, they should be still soft yet cooked through.

11. Using a sieve or perforated spoon, scoop the gnocchi directly into sauce, allowing some of the water clinging to them to come along. When all the gnocchi have been added to the sauce, cook them over medium-high heat, stirring very gently and adding a splash of the cooking water as needed if the sauce separates, until gnocchi are coated with the sauce, about 1 minute. Carefully spoon the gnocchi and sauce into serving dishes. Serve right away.

Beet and Fonio Salad with Spicy Pickled Carrots

INGREDIENTS

3 ½ pounds beets, trimmed and scrubbed

1 tablespoon extra virgin olive oil, plus more for drizzling

1 ½ cups cooked fonio

½ cup Spicy Pickled Carrots (recipe follows), drained

1 ½ cups roasted peanuts, coarsely chopped (optional)

¼ cup chopped fresh dill Vinaigrette (page 90) Kosher salt

SERVES 4

This salad has all my favorite flavors. An exquisite combination of the sweet meatiness and the dainty smoky taste of the roasted beets combines with the spicy acidity of the pickled carrots, the freshness of the dill, and the subtle earthiness of the fonio.

The salad components can each be made up to 3 days in advance and refrigerated separately until you're ready to combine them and serve. This salad can also be assembled fully up to 3 days in advance and refrigerated, as it improves with time as the fonio absorbs flavors from the dressing and other ingredients.

PREPARATION

1. Preheat the oven to 425°F.

2. Coat the beets with the oil and wrap them in aluminum foil. Roast until they are easily pierced by a fork or paring knife, about 1 hour. Let cool.

3. Peel the beets and cut into 1/2-inch pieces. Set aside if assembling the salad now, or place in a covered container in the refrigerator.

4. Combine the fonio, diced beets, pickled carrots, peanuts (if using), and dill in a large serving bowl. Toss well. Dress with enough vinaigrette to coat, drizzling on extra oil at any point to refresh the salad if it appears dry. Season with salt to taste and serve.

Spicy Pickled Carrots

These pickled carrots are great as a side or a topping. They will add a burst of fresh and spicy acidity and sweetness. They can be prepared in advance and refrigerated in their pickling juice for up to 3 days.

INGREDIENTS

6   carrots, peeled and coarsley grated

1   Scotch bonnet pepper, stemmed, seeded, and minced

½   yellow onion, finely chopped

1   tablespoon salt

1   cup light brown sugar

2   cups rice vinegar

MAKES 3 CUPS

PREPARATION

1. In a large bowl, combine the carrots, Scotch bonnet, onion, and salt and let sit for about 1 hour to draw out excess liquid.

2. Drain the liquid from the carrot mixture and squeeze well. Place the carrot mixture in a saucepan and stir in the sugar and vinegar. Bring to a boil, stirring to dissolve the sugar. Remove from the heat and cover the pot. Let sit off the heat for about 15 minutes to infuse and cool.

3. Transfer to an airtight container and refrigerate. Drain before serving.

Vinaigrette

This is my go-to dressing when I want to keep it simple. The mustard and garlic give it a robust character that is highlighted by the subtle champagne vinegar. It can be prepared ahead and stored in the refrigerator in a tightly closed jar for up to 3 days. If refrigerated, rewhisk to combine before using.

INGREDIENTS

1   teaspoon Dijon mustard

1   teaspoon minced garlic

3   tablespoons champagne vinegar

1   teaspoon salt

½   teaspoon freshly ground black pepper

½   cup extra virgin olive oil

MAKES ABOUT ¾ CUP

PREPARATION

1. In a small bowl, whisk together the mustard, garlic, vinegar, salt, and pepper. While whisking, slowly add the oil until the vinaigrette is emulsified.

MAIN COURSES

Monique's Caldou with Fonio and Sorrel-Okra Relish

INGREDIENTS

2	cups water or fish broth
½	onion, coarsely chopped
2	tablespoons peeled and chopped tomato
¼	cup lime juice
4	sea bass fillets (4 to 6 ounces each)
2	tablespoons fish sauce
1	whole Scotch bonnet pepper
	Salt and freshly ground black pepper
4	cups cooked fonio
1	cup Sorrel-Okra Relish (recipe follows)

SERVES 4

My Uncle Omi's wife, Monique Diémé, makes the best *caldou*; I always make it a point to stop by their house for my fix whenever I am in Dakar. Monique grew up in the village of Coubalan, near the town of Tobor, about 30 minutes north of Ziguinchor, on the banks of the Casamance River. Caldou has its Portuguese-sounding name because this part of Senegal neighbors Guinea Bissau, a former Portuguese colony.

Caldou is a light fish dish, usually made with carp or sea bream in Senegal, although you can use sea bass or snapper, which are easier to find in the U.S. The fish is simply poached in a broth with lime, tomato, and okra, and often served with a side of *baguedj*, a foamy-looking relish of puréed sorrel leaves and okra. Monique serves her caldou with fonio, to the delight of Uncle O and their two children, JB and Coura.

At my restaurant, I like to present this caldou, inspired by Monique's recipe. Basically, it's the same flavors presented in a more elegant way with the sauces.

PREPARATION

1. In a large skillet, bring the water to a boil over medium heat. Add the onions and cook for about 5 minutes, until soft. Add the tomatoes and cook for 10 minutes, until tomatoes are incorporated. Stir in the lime juice.

2. Gently place the fish on the simmering broth. Drizzle with the fish sauce and add the Scotch bonnet. Simmer for 5 to 6 minutes, loosely covered, until the fillets are cooked through. Transfer the fish to a platter, cover loosely with aluminum foil, and set aside to keep warm. Remove the Scotch bonnet from the broth and discard.

3. In a blender, blend the cooking broth, tomatoes, and onions until you get a smooth, bright orange sauce. Adjust the seasoning with salt and pepper.

4. To serve, place the fonio in the center of each of four plates. Generously pour the sauce around the fonio. Place a fillet on the fonio and top with a generous dollop of the relish.

Sorrel-Okra Relish (Baguedj)

INGREDIENTS

Juice of 1 lime (optional)

1 pound sorrel or spinach, trimmed

Kosher salt

5 whole okra pods, trimmed

Fish sauce (optional)

MAKES ABOUT 1 CUP

Baguedj can be kept in a tightly closed jar, refrigerated, for 2 to 3 days.

PREPARATION

1. Fill a large pot halfway with water and bring to a boil. If using spinach, add the lime juice. Add the sorrel or spinach leaves. Cook for about 5 minutes, stirring after about 2 minutes, until the leaves are cooked through and very soft. (The leaves will change color dramatically.) Drain well, let cool slightly, and squeeze out any excess water.

2. Boil the okra in enough salted water to cover for about 5 minutes, until soft. Drain well.

3. Put the leaves and okra in a food processor or blender. Process or blend until light and foamy. Add salt or fish sauce to taste.

Toasted Fonio, Black-Eyed Pea Leaf & Bean Stew

This easy dish hails from Burkina Faso. Toasting the fonio for a few minutes in a dry pan gives it a lovely smoky flavor. Black-eyed pea leaves can be substituted with spinach. An excellent side dish for grilled meat (traditionally lamb in Burkina Faso), this stew can also be served on its own as a satisfying vegetarian entree if you use dawadawa or fermented black beans, not fish sauce.

INGREDIENTS

1   cup dried kidney beans, soaked overnight and drained

2 ½ quarts cold water

     Salt and freshly ground black pepper

1   cup raw fonio

2 ½ cups water

4   cups tightly packed black-eyed pea leaves or spinach, chopped

1   tablespoon red palm oil or vegetable oil

½   cup grated onions

1   cup chopped tomatoes (canned are fine)

1   tablespoon dawadawa, fermented black beans, or fish sauce

1   bay leaf

1   cup green beans cut in 2-inch lengths

SERVES 4

PREPARATION

1. In a large pot, combine the kidney beans and cold water. Bring to a boil, reduce to a simmer, and cook until the beans are very soft. This could take 25 to 30 minutes, or much longer if the beans are old. Drain, season with 1 tablespoon salt or to taste, and set aside.

2. In a dry skillet, toast the fonio over low heat until golden, 7 to 10 minutes, stirring often to prevent scorching. Remove from the heat.

3. In a large pot, bring the 2 1/2 cups water to a boil. Add the leaves and simmer for about 5 minutes, until soft. Using a sieve or perforated spoon, scoop out the leaves and transfer them to a blender. Reserve the water in the pot. Blend the leaves to a purée and set aside.

4. Add the oil, onions, tomatoes, dawadawa (if using), bay leaf, and salt to taste to the reserved water. Bring to a simmer, then stir in the toasted fonio and the leaf purée. Cook for 15 minutes, until it forms a thick, uniform sauce. Remove the bay leaf and fold in the kidney beans. Serve hot.

Fonio, Kale & Caramelized Onion Frittata

INGREDIENTS

Kosher salt

1   bunch kale, stemmed and cut crosswise into thin shreds

Nonstick spray or vegetable oil, for greasing the skillet

2   tablespoons olive oil

1   cup thinly sliced onions

½   cup diced red bell pepper

1   garlic clove, minced

½   cup cooked fonio

4   large eggs

¼   cup milk

½   cup grated cheddar or goat cheese, plus extra for the top (optional)

1   teaspoon salt

½   teaspoon freshly ground black pepper

SERVES 4

This makes a simple and satisfying brunch dish that can be served with a salad or grilled sausages. The caramelized onions impart a sweetness that balances the bitterness of the kale.

PREPARATION

1. Bring a large pot of salted water to a boil. Add the kale and cook for about 2 minutes, until it has fully wilted. Drain in a colander and run under cold water to stop the cooking. Squeeze out excess water. You should have about 1 cup kale shreds.

2. Preheat the oven to 375°F. Spray a 9- or 10-inch heavy oven-proof skillet with vegetable oil.

3. Heat the olive oil in the skillet over medium heat. Cook the onions and bell pepper for 3 to 5 minutes, stirring occasionally, until the onions start to brown and caramelize. Add the garlic and cook for another 2 minutes. Add the kale and cook for about 5 minutes, until soft and tender. Remove from the heat and fold in the fonio.

4. In a bowl, whisk together the eggs and milk. Stir in the cheese, salt, and pepper. Pour over the fonio-vegetable mixture. If you like, sprinkle with more cheese.

5. Bake for 30 to 35 minutes, until puffed and set. (A toothpick inserted in the center should come out clean.) Serve warm, at room temperature, or cold.

Palm Nut and Vegetable Stew (Tendouran)

INGREDIENTS

2–3 pounds fresh palm nuts, or one 800-gram can palm nut concentrate

Boiling water

1 pound cassava (yucca), peeled and cut into 2-inch chunks

1 pound carrots, peeled and cut into 2-inch chunks

1 eggplant (about 1 pound), cut into 2-inch chunks

1 whole Scotch bonnet pepper

Salt and freshly ground black pepper

½ pound okra pods, trimmed and thinly sliced

8 cups cooked fonio

SPECIAL EQUIPMENT
Mortar and pestle

SERVES 4

Another treat from Mañima Camara. She prepares the palm nuts from scratch, but there are good canned options that can be bought in African grocery stores or online (see Resources). This stew can be eaten with plain cooked fonio. Be generous with the sauce, as fonio loves to absorb sauces.

PREPARATION

1. If using fresh palm nuts: In a large pot, cover the palm nuts with water by 2 inches and bring to a boil. Reduce to a simmer and cook for 20 minutes, until the oil rises to the surface.

2. Drain the nuts and discard the water and oil. Using a mortar and pestle and working in batches if necessary, lightly pound the nuts to separate the red pulp; discard the hard seed in the middle. Transfer the pounded nuts to a heatproof container.

3. Pour in enough boiling water to cover the palm nuts and mix well. Let sit for 30 minutes. Strain the resulting liquid through a colander into a large pot. Squeeze the pulp well and discard the remaining seeds and fibers (see Note).

4. If using canned palm nut concentrate, pour it into a large pot.

5. Add the cassava, carrots, eggplant, and Scotch bonnet to the palm nut liquid or concentrate. Add water if necessary to cover the vegetables. Bring to a boil, then reduce to a simmer. Season with salt and pepper and cook for about 15 minutes, until the vegetables are tender.

6. Add the okra and simmer for another 5 to 7 minutes, until the okra is just soft. Serve the stew hot over the fonio.

Note: The palm nut fibers are sometimes mixed with honey and given to kids as a snack.

Fonio with Beef, Palm Nuts & Baobab Leaf Sauce (Naada)

This is a simple, delicious stew prepared with essentially two key ingredients: palm nuts and baobab leaves. In Sedhiou, the beef is optional; you can also use fish and/or vegetables.

INGREDIENTS

2–3 pounds fresh palm nuts, or one 800-gram can palm nut concentrate

Boiling water

3 pounds boneless beef shoulder, cut into 2-inch pieces

Salt and freshly ground black pepper

2 cups baobab leaf powder (lalo)

6 cups cooked fonio

SPECIAL EQUIPMENT
Mortar and pestle

SERVES 4

PREPARATION

1. If using fresh palm nuts: In a large pot, cover the palm nuts with water by 2 inches and bring to a boil. Reduce to a simmer and cook for 20 minutes, until the oil rises to the surface.

2. Drain the nuts and discard the water and oil. Using a mortar and pestle and working in batches if necessary, lightly pound the nuts to separate the red pulp; discard the hard seed in the middle. Transfer the pounded nuts to a heatproof container.

3. Pour in enough boiling water to cover the palm nuts and mix well. Let sit for 30 minutes. Strain the resulting liquid through a colander into a large pot. Squeeze the pulp well and discard the remaining seeds and fibers.

4. If using canned palm nut concentrate, pour it into a large pot.

5. Add the beef to the palm nut liquid or concentrate and bring to a boil. Reduce the heat and simmer for about 2 hours, until the beef is tender.

6. Season with salt and pepper. Sprinkle with the baobab powder and stir well. Cook for another 5 minutes, until the sauce starts to thicken, then turn off the heat. Let sit for about 10 minutes, stirring once, until the sauce thickens. Serve with the cooked fonio.

Fonio & Sweet Potato Crab Cakes with Spicy Papaya-Lime Sauce

I love crab cakes. This version–with the earthy fonio, sweet potatoes, fruity papaya, tangy lime, spicy Scotch bonnet, and crunchy cornmeal–brings a unique flavor to the crab. Served with a salad, it becomes a light yet complete meal.

PREPARATION

1. Prepare the crab cakes: Bring a pot of salted water to a boil. Add the sweet potatoes and cook until tender and easily pierced with a fork, about 10 minutes. Drain well and transfer to a large bowl. Mash the sweet potatoes until smooth. Let cool to room temperature.

2. Add the egg and egg yolk to the sweet potatoes and beat to mix thoroughly. Stir in the bell pepper, fonio, cornmeal, scallion, parsley, lemon juice, mayonnaise, black pepper, mustard, and cumin. Fold in the crab. Form into 12 cakes and sprinkle with the salt. Place on a platter, cover lightly, and refrigerate until you're ready to cook them.

3. Prepare the sauce: In a blender, blend the papaya, green onion, cilantro, lime juice, garlic, Scotch bonnet, and salt until it's mashed but still slightly chunky. Transfer to a serving bowl, adjust the seasoning with salt, and set aside.

4. Line a platter with paper towels. Heat the oil in a large skillet over medium heat until shimmering. Add the crab cakes in batches and fry for 3 to 4 minutes on each side, until golden brown. Transfer the crab cakes to the paper towels to drain briefly.

5. Serve the crab cakes topped with the sauce.

INGREDIENTS

For the Crab Cakes

Kosher salt

1 large sweet potato (about 1 pound), peeled and cut into 2-inch chunks

1 large egg plus 1 large egg yolk

1 green bell pepper, stemmed, seeded, and finely chopped

½ cup cooked fonio

¼ cup cornmeal

1 scallion (white part only), chopped

2 tablespoons minced fresh flat-leaf parsley

2 tablespoons lemon juice

2 tablespoons mayonnaise

1 teaspoon freshly ground black pepper

2 teaspoons Dijon mustard

1½ teaspoons ground cumin

2 cups lump crabmeat (about 10 ounces), picked over for cartilage and shells

½ teaspoon salt

¼ cup vegetable oil

SERVES 4

For the Papaya-Lime Sauce

1 cup chopped peeled papaya

¼ cup chopped scallions

1 tablespoon chopped fresh cilantro

1 teaspoon lime juice

½ teaspoon minced garlic

½ Scotch bonnet pepper, stemmed, seeded, and minced

¼ teaspoon salt

Seafood & Okra Stew (Soupou Kanja)

INGREDIENTS

	About 24 littleneck or manila clams
3	quarts fish or vegetable broth
3	bay leaves
2	yellow onions, coarsely chopped
4	tablespoons fish sauce
2	habanero or Scotch bonnet chiles, slit in half lengthwise
16	medium shrimp, peeled and deveined
6	tablespoons red palm oil
8	cups thinly sliced okra (about 3 pounds untrimmed)
	Freshly ground black pepper
6	cups cooked fonio

SERVES 6 TO 8

The Middle Passage, as the transatlantic slave trade is known, brought numerous West African culinary traditions to the Americas. This dish is the ancestor of gumbo. Sometimes in southern Senegal, it is served with fonio instead of rice.

PREPARATION

1. Place the clams in a colander in the sink under cold running water. Scrub with a brush to remove grit. Gently tap any open clams with your fingers; discard any that do not close. Set aside in the refrigerator.

2. Bring the broth to a boil in a large saucepan over high heat. Add the bay leaves and onions. Reduce heat to medium-low and cook until the broth has reduced by one-quarter, about 20 minutes.

3. Add 3 tablespoons of the fish sauce and the chiles to the broth. Cook, stirring occasionally, for 10 minutes, until the onions have almost dissolved in the broth.

4. Add the clams and shrimp. Cover the pan and cook until the clams open and shrimp are cooked through, about 4 minutes. Discard any clams that have not opened by this time.

5. Add the oil and okra and stir once. Cook for 3 to 5 minutes, until the okra is tender.

6. Remove from heat and stir in the remaining 1 tablespoon fish sauce and pepper to taste. Remove the bay leaves. Divide the fonio evenly among six to eight bowls and ladle the stew over it. Serve immediately.

Tamarind Roast Chicken with Fonio & Roasted Cauliflower Pilaf

INGREDIENTS

For the Tamarind Roast Chicken

1   whole chicken (2 ½ to 3 pounds), rinsed and dried thoroughly

     Kosher salt and freshly ground black pepper

1½   cups Tamarind Sauce (page 62)

2–3 tablespoons water

For the Fonio & Toasted Cauliflower Pilaf

1   head cauliflower (about 2 pounds), broken into florets

2   tablespoons medium-hot curry powder

3   tablespoons vegetable oil

1   onion, chopped

2   garlic cloves, crushed and peeled

     2-inch piece ginger, grated

2   tablespoons garam masala

3   curry leaves

4   cups cooked fonio

1   teaspoon salt

     Handful of fresh cilantro, chopped

     Grated zest of 1 lemon

½   cup roasted cashew nuts, chopped

SERVES 4

Although the spices used in this recipe are inspired by Indian cooking, this dish also has flavors familiar to my home cooking, in particular tamarind, which in Wolof (one of Senegal's national languages) is called *dakhar,* as in Dakar, Senegal.

The curried spiced pilaf is vegetarian and can be eaten on its own or with yogurt, as a great side. You can even use it as stuffing for the chicken. Note that the chicken requires marinating for 2 hours or overnight. In the finished sauce, you should be able to taste the fermented flavor from the fish sauce, the sweetness from the honey, acidity from the tamarind, and the heat from the chili.

PREPARATION

1. Marinate the chicken: Season the chicken generously with salt and place it in a roasting pan. Coat the cavity and outside liberally with all of the tamarind sauce. Marinate for 2 hours at room temperature or overnight in the refrigerator.

2. Prepare the pilaf: Heat the oven to 400°F.

3. In a large bowl, toss the cauliflower with the curry powder and 2 tablespoons of the oil. Season with salt and spread out on a rimmed baking sheet. Roast for about 25 minutes, stirring occasionally, until golden brown and tender. Remove from the oven and set aside. Turn the oven up to 425°F for the chicken.

4. Heat the remaining 1 tablespoon oil in a large skillet over medium-high heat. Add the onion and cook for 5 minutes, until golden. Add the garlic, ginger, and garam masala and cook for 5 minutes more, until fragrant. Add the curry leaves. Fold in the cooked fonio. Remove from the heat and let cool for 5 minutes.

5. Gently stir in the roasted cauliflower, cilantro, lemon zest, and cashews. Cover and set aside to keep warm, or allow it to cool to room temperature.

6. To roast the chicken: If the chicken was refrigerated, remove it from the fridge when you start roasting the cauliflower.

7. Turn the chicken on its side and roast for 20 minutes, until brown. Turn the chicken onto its other side and roast for another 20 minutes. Finally, turn the chicken onto its back, baste it with the fat that has dripped into the pan, and roast for 10 minutes more, until the skin over the breast is brown and an instant-read thermometer inserted into the thickest part of the inner thigh reads between 165° and 180°F.

8. Transfer the chicken to a cutting board, cover loosely with foil, and let rest for 10 to 15 minutes.

9. While the chicken rests, add the water to the roasting pan and place it over medium heat. Scrape with a spatula or wooden spoon to dissolve and loosen the browned drippings. Transfer the pan juices to a heat-proof bowl. Let stand briefly, then skim off and discard most of the fat, leaving the flavorful pan juices.

10. Carve the chicken into serving pieces and transfer to a platter. Drizzle the pan juices over the chicken. Serve the pilaf on the side.

Note: For a vegetarian option, omit the chicken as pictured here.

Monique & Augustine's Chicken Yassa

The Diémé sisters, Monique and Augustine, are nicknamed *saf loxo* (flavorful hands) in their Mbao neighborhood. Mbao is located in the suburbs of Dakar, and although driving there can take a couple of hours because of the heavy traffic, the Diémé sisters' chicken *yassa*, a classic Senegalese dish, is definitely worth the trip. This chicken is served with an onion and lime sauce, cooked slowly until the onion caramelizes and imparts a sweetness that balances the tartness of the lime. This sweet and tart sauce goes perfectly well with the charred chicken, although *yassa* can also be prepared with fish.

INGREDIENTS

6	bone-in, skinless whole chicken legs, cut apart into thighs and drumsticks
2	tablespoons fresh thyme, finely chopped
4	scallions, finely chopped
¾	(about) cup lime juice (6 to 7 limes)
1	tablespoon white vinegar
¼	cup peanut or vegetable oil
2	pounds yellow onions, cut in thick strips
1	whole Scotch bonnet pepper
1	bay leaf
1½	teaspoons Dijon mustard
1	tablespoon salt
½	teaspoon freshly ground black pepper
2	tablespoons Nokos (recipe follows)
1	cup water
½	cup green olives, rinsed
	Spring Vegetable Fonio Pilaf (page 76), for serving

SERVES 6

PREPARATION

1. In a large bowl, combine the chicken pieces, thyme, scallions, about 1/4 cup of the lime juice, the vinegar, and 1 tablespoon of the oil. Mix well so the chicken is thoroughly coated. Cover and marinate in the fridge for at least 2 hours or overnight.

2. Heat a grill until hot. Remove the chicken from the marinade; discard the remaining marinade. Grill the chicken until it's almost cooked through, 6 to 7 minutes on each side. (It will finish cooking in the onion sauce, imparting to the sauce its lovely grill flavors.) Transfer the chicken to a platter, cover loosely with aluminum foil, and set aside.

3. Meanwhile, in a large pot, heat the remaining 3 tablespoons oil over medium-high heat. When the oil is hot, add the onions and cook for 1 to 2 minutes without stirring. Stir once with a wooden spoon, then allow the onions to begin caramelizing. Only stir from time to time to avoid scorching, but make sure to allow the onions to get some color, 10 to 12 minutes.

4. Stir in the Scotch bonnet, bay leaf, and mustard. Continue cooking and stirring for about 5 minutes, until the pepper is slightly fragrant and the onions have a uniform light brown color; add 1 to 2 tablespoons water only as needed to avoid scorching.

5. Add the remaining lime juice to taste. Season with the salt and pepper. Add the nokos, the grilled chicken, any juices that have accumulated in the platter, and the 1 cup water. Stir well. Simmer until chicken is completely cooked through, 10 to 15 minutes. Add the olives.

6. Remove the bay leaf and the Scotch bonnet (if you don't want to serve it). Serve the chicken and sauce over the pilaf.

Author Pierre Thiam with Monique Diémé.

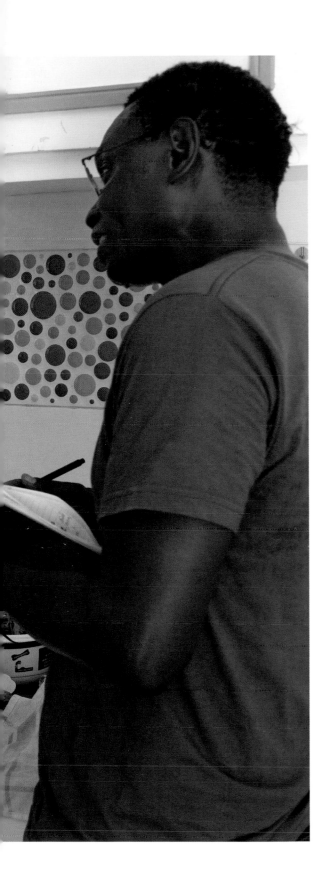

Nokos

INGREDIENTS

2   bay leaves

2   green jalapeño or other chiles, stemmed and chopped

1   small green bell pepper, stemmed, seeded and chopped

¼   cup whole black peppercorns

1   head garlic, separated into cloves and peeled

1   tablespoon grated fresh ginger

SPECIAL EQUIPMENT
High-powered blender such as a Vitamix, or food processor

MAKES 1 CUP

Nokos is a classic Senegalese seasoning. Just a little bit of nokos, added toward the end, can revive a sauce or stew, brightening up flavors that have started to fade from lengthy cooking, much like a spritz of lemon. Store in a tightly covered jar in the refrigerator for up to 2 weeks.

PREPARATION

1. Combine all the ingredients in a blender and process until it forms a thick, wet paste.

Fonio with Shrimp & Kimchi Stir-Fry

INGREDIENTS

1	tablespoon vegetable oil
4	teaspoons sesame oil
1	tablespoon chopped garlic
1	tablespoon chopped fresh ginger
1	pound medium shrimp, peeled and deveined
4	teaspoons sesame seeds
1	teaspoon soy sauce
1	teaspoon sweet soy sauce
2	cups kimchi, drained
1	small leaf napa cabbage, sliced crosswise into 1-inch strips (about ½ cup)
½	cup coarsely grated carrots
1	teaspoon minced seeded jalapeño chile
2	teaspoons fish sauce
6	cups cooked fonio, at room temperature

SERVES 4

Although I am not a big fan of the word "fusion" when it comes to cooking, many of our foods come from the meeting of cultures. This stir-fry is a wonderful pairing of Korean and West African influences. Vegetarians and vegans can skip the shrimp.

PREPARATION

1. Heat the vegetable oil and sesame oil in a wok over medium heat. Add the garlic and ginger and stir-fry until fragrant, about 1 minute. Add shrimp and stir-fry until almost cooked through, 2 to 3 minutes.

2. Add the sesame seeds, soy sauce, sweet soy sauce, and kimchi and stir-fry until the kimchi is hot. Add the cabbage and carrots and stir-fry for 1 minute more. Add the jalapeño and season with the fish sauce. Add the fonio and stir well until it is heated through. Serve immediately.

Fonio, Grilled Lamb Chops & Asparagus with Mafé Sauce

INGREDIENTS

For the Mafe Sauce

1	tablespoon peanut or vegetable oil
1	onion, finely chopped
1	tablespoon tomato paste
2	cups unsweetened smooth peanut butter
1	quart chicken broth
1	whole Scotch bonnet pepper (optional)

For the Lamb and Asparagus

8	lamb chops, trimmed of excess fat
2	tablespoons vegetable oil
2	tablespoons chopped fresh thyme
2	teaspoons minced garlic
	Salt
½	teaspoon freshly ground black pepper
1	pound green asparagus, trimmed
5	cups cooked fonio

SERVES 4

Mafé is the name for peanut sauce in Senegal. To me, it is the ultimate comfort food and one of my favorite sauces to eat with fonio. I like it mildly spicy. You can add chopped okra, which adds a bit more rich, thick texture to the sauce. Here, I serve it simply with lamb chops and grilled asparagus, but mafé is a versatile sauce so the choice of meat and vegetables can vary.

This particular recipe was inspired by a dish prepared by Mañima Camara (see page 39) when I visited her in Hainou Salam, a lush and peaceful hamlet located in Sedhiou in South Senegal, a region that is considered the breadbasket of Senegal.

PREPARATION

1. Prepare the mafé sauce: In a large pot, heat the oil over medium-high heat. Add the onion and cook until soft but not brown, 3 to 5 minutes. Add the tomato paste and reduce the heat to low. Stirring with a wooden spoon, cook for about 5 minutes, until the tomato paste is deep red. Add a few tablespoons water only if necessary to avoid scorching.

2. Add the peanut butter and stir well to combine. Add chicken broth and bring to a boil. Add the Scotch bonnet (if using). Reduce the heat to a simmer and stir periodically to dissolve the peanut butter in the liquid. Cook for 15 to 20 minutes, until oil rises to the surface. Remove from the heat and keep warm.

3. Prepare the lamb and vegetables: Preheat the grill to high heat. Rub the lamb chops all over with the oil, thyme, garlic, 1 teaspoon salt, and the pepper. Grill for about 5 minutes on each side, until nicely browned and medium; cook for more or less time, depending on the thickness, or for a different doneness.

4. Set the lamb chops on a platter, cover loosely with aluminum foil, and let rest for 5 minutes.

5. While the lamb rests, season the asparagus with salt and grill them for about 3 minutes, turning occasionally, until nicely charred.

6. Serve with the lamb and fonio with a generous amount of sauce.

Beef & Fonio Meatballs with Sweet Potato Stew

The sauce for this dish is known as *thiou* in Senegal, where the meatballs are usually prepared with ground beef or chicken without fonio. Here in New York, I've been playing with new meatball mixtures and find that fonio gives lightness to the meatballs while the parmesan, not traditional in Senegal, adds umami. This dish is great when served with bread to scoop up the tomato sauce, or with rice or pasta.

INGREDIENTS

Kosher salt

½ pound sweet potato, peeled and cut into 1-inch chunks

3 tablespoons peanut or vegetable oil

2 large onions, finely chopped

4 garlic cloves, crushed, peeled, and minced

1 bay leaf

2 cups chopped tomatoes

2 cups chicken broth

1½ teaspoons salt

½ teaspoon freshly ground black pepper

1 pound lean ground beef

2 cups cooked fonio

¼ cup grated parmesan cheese

1 large egg

2 tablespoons chopped fresh thyme

SERVES 4

PREPARATION

1. In a large pot with boiling salted water, cook the sweet potatoes for about 5 minutes, until softened slightly but still firm. Drain and set aside.

2. Prepare the sauce: Heat 2 tablespoons of the oil in a large skillet over medium heat. Add half of the onions, half the garlic, and the bay leaf and cook until the onions are soft, about 6 minutes. Add the tomatoes, 1 cup of the chicken broth, 1 teaspoon of the salt and 1/4 teaspoon of the pepper. Reduce the heat to a simmer and cook for 15 to 20 minutes, until the sauce has the thickness of marinara. Turn off the heat.

3. Prepare the meatballs: In a large bowl, mix together the ground beef, fonio, the remaining onion, remaining garlic, parmesan, egg, thyme, the remaining 1/2 teaspoon salt and the remaining 1/4 teaspoon pepper until well combined. Shape into 16 balls the size of golf balls. Refrigerate for an hour or until you're ready to cook.

4. In a skillet, heat the remaining 1 tablespoon oil over medium-high heat. Add the meatballs in batches, without crowding the pan. Cook for about 10 minutes, turning them occasionally, until nicely brown on all sides. As they finish cooking, add them to the sauce.

5. Add a little water to the sauce if necessary to almost cover the meatballs. Simmer gently, covered, for about 25 minutes. Add the sweet potatoes and simmer about another 5 minutes, until the meatballs are firm and the sweet potatoes are cooked through. Remove the lid and cook for 5 to 7 minutes more, until the sauce is reduced and thick. Serve hot.

Fonio Thiebou Djenn

This dish is also known as *fini zame* in Mali, *founden yolifebande* in Guinea, or simply *fonio "au gras"* in Burkina Faso. Similar to the Senegalese tomato-rich version of *jollof* rice, here fonio is used in place of rice. Traditionally, it is served hot with the fonio at the bottom of the shared platter, with vegetables and fish as centerpieces, and the whole dish ladled with broth.

INGREDIENTS

1 whole grouper, red snapper, or sea bass (about 3 pounds), filleted and cut into 4 pieces; reserve head and bones

½ cup vegetable oil

Rof (recipe follows)

Salt and freshly ground black pepper

2 white onions, chopped

1 green bell pepper, stemmed, seeded, and chopped

2 cups tomato paste

5 cups water

½ head green cabbage, cut into 4 wedges

1 cup dried white hibiscus flowers (bisaap; optional)

1 Scotch bonnet pepper

2 tablespoons fish sauce

1 small butternut squash, peeled, seeded, and cut into large chunks

2 whole bitter eggplants (diaxatou; optional)

¼ pound whole okra pods, trimmed

Soaked and strained pulp from 1 handful tamarind pods (see Tamarind Sauce, page 62, for preparation) or 1 tablespoon tamarind paste (optional)

4 cups cooked fonio

2 limes, cut into wedges

SERVES 4

PREPARATION

1. Cut two 2-inch-long slits in each fish fillet and stuff with about 1 teaspoon rof. Coat the fish with the remaining rof. Set aside.

2. Heat the vegetable oil in a large pot over medium-high heat. Add 2 pinches salt, the onions, green pepper, and tomato paste. Reduce the heat to low and stir well. Stirring occasionally to avoid scorching, cook for 10 to 15 minutes, until the vegetables are soft and the tomato paste turns a dark orange. Add the water and stir well. The paste will thin, becoming sauce-like. Return to a boil and simmer for about 30 minutes.

3. Add the fish head and bones to the pot along with the cabbage, hibiscus (if using), Scotch bonnet, and a pinch of black pepper. Cook uncovered for about 30 minutes over medium heat.

4. Carefully remove the fish head and bones from the pot and discard. Add the fish sauce to the broth. Partially cover the pot, leaving the lid ajar, and simmer for 10 minutes.

5. Add the butternut squash and the bitter eggplants (if using). Return to a boil and season with salt and pepper. Reduce the heat and simmer for another 10 minutes.

6. Add the okra and cook for another 5 minutes. By now, all the vegetables should be tender. Remove the cabbage wedges, Scotch bonnet, squash, and eggplants from the pot and place them in a bowl with a couple of ladles of the broth. Keep warm.

7. Add the fish fillets to the remaining broth and simmer for about 10 minutes, until cooked through. Carefully remove the fish and add the fillets to the vegetables. Spoon the tamarind pulp over the fish and vegetables.

8. Use a ladle to skim excess oil from the top of the broth; discard the oil.

9. Off the heat, fold the fonio into the broth until it has absorbed the broth and is bright red. Spread the fonio on a large platter. Arrange the fish and vegetables evenly over the fonio. Serve with lime wedges.

Rof

Rof, pronounced "rawf," is a popular condiment in Senegal, commonly used to stuff fish.

INGREDIENTS

1   bunch parsley, coarsely chopped

1   habanero chile, stemmed and coarsely chopped

3   garlic cloves, peeled

1   onion, chopped, or 1 small bunch scallions, white parts only, chopped

1   bay leaf, crumbled

     Salt and freshly ground black pepper

SPECIAL EQUIPMENT
Food processor or mortar and pestle

MAKES ABOUT 1 CUP

PREPARATION

1. Place the parsley, habanero, garlic, onion, and bay leaf in a food processor or mortar. Process until chopped coarsely, or pound by hand with a pestle to a rough paste. Season to taste with salt and pepper.

Fonio and Seafood "Paella"

INGREDIENTS

	About 16 mussels
1	small onion, chopped
2	tablespoons olive oil
1	garlic clove, minced
1	teaspoon red curry powder
2	tablespoons tomato paste
2	cups chopped tomatoes
1	quart fish or chicken broth, plus more if needed
12	whole shell-on jumbo shrimp
4	scallops, cleaned
4	cleaned small squid, bodies sliced into ¼-inch-wide rings, tentacles left whole
	Salt
4	cups cooked fonio
1	cup frozen peas
4	lemon wedges, for garnish

SERVES 4

To me, a Spanish paella is simply a less flavorful version of the Senegalese *thiebou jenn*. The similarities are not a coincidence, since the Moors were the first to bring rice to Valencia in the 16th century. In Southern Senegal, fonio is sometimes a substitute for rice in preparing *jollof*. I add curry spices to the seasoning and turn it into a "paella" by adding peas and seafood.

The choice of seafood is up to you. Lobster, crayfish, or octopus make great substitutes.

PREPARATION

1. Place the mussels in a colander in the sink under cold running water. Scrub with a brush to remove grit. Sometimes, the mussel comes with a beard, which can be removed by pulling it out or by simply using a knife. Gently try to close any open mussels with your fingers, or gently tap on a counter; discard any that do not close. Set aside in the refrigerator.

2. Fry the onion in the oil in a large paella pan or skillet over medium heat until soft, 3 to 4 minutes, stirring often. Stir in the garlic for 1 to 2 minutes. Before it begins to color, add the curry powder, tomato paste, and chopped tomatoes. Cook until the tomatoes are reduced and thickened and the oil rises to the surface.

3. Pour the broth into the tomato sauce and stir well. Cook over low heat for 18 to 20 minutes, until thick.

4. Add the shrimp and scallops. Cook for another few minutes, until the shrimp have just turned pink.

5. Add the squid and cook, stirring, for about 1 minute, until the squid is cooked through and turns opaque.

6. Remove the cooked shrimp, scallops, and squid with some sauce. Set aside and cover to keep warm.

7. Adjust the seasoning with salt. Fold the fonio and peas into the sauce and cook for another 2 minutes to heat through.

8. Heat about 1 inch water in a saucepan. Add the mussels, cover the pan, and cook for about 4 minutes. Discard any mussels that have not opened by this time.

9. To serve family-style, as we would in Senegal, arrange the mussels, scallops, shrimp, and squid on top of the fonio and garnish with the lemon. Or serve the seafood and fonio in separate bowls. Serve any extra seafood that does not fit in the pan on the side.

Squid Ink Fonio & Piri Piri Prawns

In this dish, the fonio grains act as great mini sponges for liquid, marvelously sopping up the squid ink sauce. The piri piri heat opens up your palate to better savor the curry spices and rich briny flavor of squid ink which, despite the name, can come from squid, octopus, or cuttlefish. I also love the beautiful dark hue it imparts to the dish, and only a few drops go a long way. Squid ink can be bought online or at gourmet grocery stores.

INGREDIENTS

For the Piri Piri Prawns

¼ cup plus 1 tablespoon vegetable oil

Juice of 1 lemon

Juice of ½ lime

1 habanero chile, stemmed, seeded, and chopped

1 teaspoon tomato paste

2 garlic cloves, minced

4 tablespoons chopped cilantro

1 teaspoon kosher salt

2 pounds shell-on prawns or shrimp

For the Squid Ink Fonio

¼ cup olive oil

1 onion, chopped

1 tablespoon hot red curry powder

1 clove garlic, sliced

1 teaspoon squid ink

1 cup diced peeled tomatoes (canned are fine)

2 cups fish broth or water

Salt and freshly ground black pepper

4 cups cooked fonio

1 scallion, shredded or chopped

Lime wedges, for serving

SERVES 4

PREPARATION

1. Prepare the prawns: Combine 1/4 cup of the vegetable oil, the lemon juice, lime juice, habanero, tomato paste, and garlic in a bowl and mix well. Transfer to a small skillet and cook over medium-high heat until reduced by half, about 5 minutes. Remove from heat and let cool.

2. Stir in 3 tablespoons of the cilantro and the salt. Put the prawns in a large bowl, add the marinade, and stir to coat well. Cover and refrigerate for up to 1 hour.

3. Heat the remaining 1 tablespoon vegetable oil in a large skillet over high heat until very hot. Add the prawns and marinade and cook, tossing often, until shrimp are cooked through and the sauce has thickened, about 5 minutes. Remove from the heat and set aside to keep warm.

4. Prepare the squid ink fonio: Gently cook the onion on medium heat in olive oil until soft and slightly golden, 3 to 5 minutes. Add the curry powder and stir until fragrant, about 1 minute. Add the garlic and the squid ink. Cook for a few minutes, until the mixture is strikingly black. Add the tomatoes and cook for 5 minutes, until the tomatoes start to break down. Add the fish broth and season with 1 teaspoon salt and 1/2 teaspoon pepper. Let simmer gently, covered, for 30 minutes, stirring occasionally, until the liquid is jet black and thick. If needed, add some more water to the pan to keep it saucy.

5. Gradually add the fonio to the sauce, stirring to incorporate well, until it has the consistency of risotto, about 5 minutes.

6. Adjust seasoning with salt and pepper if needed. Transfer the fonio to a serving dish. Arrange the shrimp on top and garnish with the scallion. Serve immediately with the lime wedges and remaining cilantro.

Roasted Salmon with Cheesy Fonio Grits

INGREDIENTS

For the Cheesy Fonio Grits

1	quart vegetable broth or water
1	garlic clove, minced
1	cup raw fonio
4	ounces extra sharp cheddar cheese, shredded (about 1½ cups)
4	tablespoons unsalted butter
2	tablespoons heavy cream
	Kosher salt and freshly ground black pepper

For the Roasted Salmon

4	skinless salmon fillets (6 ounces each, about 1 inch thick)
2	tablespoons vegetable oil
2	tablespoons chopped dill
4	poached eggs, for serving (optional)

SERVES 4

This recipe draws inspiration from shrimp and grits, a Southern classic, with salmon fillets in place of shrimp and fonio in place of grits. For an even heartier dish, add a poached egg.

PREPARATION

1. Prepare the grits: Bring the vegetable broth to a boil in a saucepan. Add the garlic and slowly stir in the fonio. Reduce the heat to medium-low and cook, stirring frequently, until the fonio grains are tender, 5 minutes. Remove from the heat and fluff the fonio with a fork. Stir in the cheese, butter, and cream. Season to taste with salt and pepper, cover, and set aside to keep warm.

2. Prepare the salmon: Season the salmon fillets with salt and pepper. Heat the oil in a large skillet over medium-high heat. When the oil is hot, add 2 of the salmon fillets and sear for 4 minutes, until golden. Flip the fish with a spatula and cook on the other side for 1 minute more for medium-rare, or 2 to 3 minutes if you prefer it medium or well-done. Remove from the pan and keep warm while you cook the other 2 salmon fillets in the same manner.

3. Divide the grits among four plates and top with the salmon and dill. Serve as is or with a poached egg on top.

BREAKFASTS & DESSERTS

Fonio & Plantain Pancakes

These pancakes make a great sugar-free, gluten-free brunch item. They're fantastic served with savory fare such as fried chicken or eggs, or they can make a sweet breakfast treat when topped with hibiscus or maple syrup.

INGREDIENTS

1   large ripe plantain, peeled and cut into 1-inch chunks or grated

1   cup cooked fonio

4   large eggs

1   teaspoon vanilla extract

¼   teaspoon baking soda

⅛   teaspoon salt

3   tablespoons coconut oil or unsalted butter, for cooking

Hibiscus Syrup (recipe follows) or maple syrup, for serving (optional)

SERVES 4

PREPARATION

1. Combine the plantain, fonio, eggs, vanilla, baking soda, and salt in a bowl. Mix with a whisk or electric mixer until you have a smooth batter.

2. Melt a little of the oil in a small skillet over medium heat. When the pan is hot, working in batches, pour 1/3 cup batter into the pan per pancake. Cook until the bottom of the pancake is golden brown. Flip and cook the other side for 1 to 2 minutes, until the pancake is cooked through. Transfer to a warm plate. Cook the rest of the pancakes in the same manner, adding more oil to the pan as needed. Serve with hibiscus syrup or maple syrup, if you like.

Hibiscus Syrup

Any leftover syrup can be stored in an airtight container in the fridge for up to 2 weeks.

INGREDIENTS

2   cups water

1   cup sugar

¾   cup dried red hibiscus flowers

MAKES ABOUT 2 CUPS

PREPARATION

1. In a pot, bring the water, sugar, and dried hibiscus to a boil over medium heat. Reduce the heat to low and simmer for 15 minutes, until liquid is syrupy.

2. Remove from the heat and let cool completely. Strain the syrup and discard the flowers. The syrup can be used immediately.

Creamy Fonio Cereal with Blueberries, Pomegranate & Brown Butter

INGREDIENTS

1	cup raw fonio
2	cups water
1	teaspoon salt
2	cups milk or full-fat coconut milk, warmed
2	teaspoons brown sugar (optional)
1	teaspoon ground cinnamon (optional)
½	cup blueberries
½	cup pomegranate seeds
2	tablespoons unsalted butter

SERVES 4

Fonio is excellent for breakfast: It is easy to digest and slowly releases energy in your body throughout the day. The choice of fruits is up to you; feel free to substitute those in the recipe with your favorite seasonal fresh fruits. The brown butter is also optional, though it will definitely add a rich, nutty flavor to your breakfast.

PREPARATION

1. Combine the fonio, water, and salt in a saucepan. Bring to a boil over high heat. Reduce the heat, cover, and simmer gently for 5 minutes, stirring occasionally, until the water has been absorbed. Turn off the heat.

2. Add the milk and stir to combine. Let stand for 1 minute. Stir in brown sugar and cinnamon (if using). Divide the fonio among four bowls and top with the blueberries and pomegranate seeds.

3. In a small pan, cook the butter until it becomes slightly brown and foamy. Drizzle over the fonio and serve.

Overnight Fonio with Coconut, Blueberries & Cashews

As with overnight oats, this breakfast is convenient as it is prepared ahead of time. The blueberries will give a lovely purple hue to this healthy dish. Plums or mango are delicious substitutes.

PREPARATION

1. Mix the fonio with the coconut and coconut water in a bowl. Cover and let sit in the fridge overnight.

2. In the morning, stir in the cashew butter. Divide among four bowls. Top with the cashews, maple syrup (if using), the blueberries, lemon zest, and cinnamon and serve.

INGREDIENTS

2   cups raw fonio

1   tablespoon unsweetened shredded coconut

2   cups coconut water

2   tablespoons cashew butter

3   tablespoons cashew nuts, coarsely crushed

1   tablespoon maple syrup (optional)

1   cup blueberries

½   teaspoon grated lemon zest

½   teaspoon ground cinnamon

SERVES 4

Mango & Fonio Muffins

These muffins are great with tea or coffee in the morning. They can be prepared ahead and kept covered at room temperatures for 1 to 2 days or refrigerated for up to 1 week.

INGREDIENTS

1	cup peeled, cubed mango (about 1 medium mango)
3	large eggs, at room temperature
2	tablespoons unsalted butter, melted
2	teaspoons lime juice
2	teaspoons vanilla extract
3	tablespoons honey
2	tablespoons cooked fonio
⅓	cup fonio flour
¼	teaspoon salt
¼	teaspoon baking soda
⅓	cup raw cashew nuts, coarsely chopped (optional)
	Grated zest of 2 limes

MAKES 8 MUFFINS

PREPARATION

1. Preheat the oven 350° F. Line 8 cups of a standard muffin tin with paper muffin cups.

2. Purée the mangoes in a food processor until creamy. Add the eggs, butter, lime juice, vanilla, and honey and pulse to combine. Add the cooked fonio, fonio flour, salt, and baking soda and process until combined in a smooth batter. If using, stir the cashews into the batter with a spoon. Fill each lined muffin tin cup almost to the top with batter.

3. Bake the muffins for 10 minutes, then place a piece of aluminum foil over the top of the muffin tin and bake for 15 minutes more or until a toothpick inserted into the center of a muffin comes out clean.

4. Set the pan on a wire rack to cool for 10 to 15 minutes, then remove the muffins from the pan and let them cool for 5 minutes directly on the rack. Sprinkle lime zest on top of each muffin and serve.

Fonio, Almond & Mango Crisp

INGREDIENTS

For Mango Filling

4	cups diced mango (2 to 3 large or 4 medium mangoes)
3½	tablespoons almond flour
1	tablespoon lemon juice

For the Fonio-Almond Topping

¾	cup cooked fonio
½	cup brown sugar
6	tablespoons almond flour
6	tablespoons sliced almonds
¾	teaspoon ground cinnamon
6	tablespoons unsalted butter, cold

SERVES 5

The simplicity of this dessert makes it look and taste like comfort food. While it's already fantastic on its own, it's also great with whipped cream or vanilla ice cream.

PREPARATION

1. Preheat oven to 350°F.

2. Prepare the filling: Put the mangoes in a 3-quart baking dish. Sprinkle the almond flour on top, then toss to evenly coat. Drizzle with the lemon juice.

3. Prepare the topping: In a bowl, combine the fonio, sugar, almond flour, sliced almonds, and cinnamon. Stir together with a fork. Cut the butter into cubes and add to the bowl. Use your fingers to combine the ingredients until crumbly.

4. Sprinkle the topping evenly over the mangoes. Bake for 35 to 40 minutes, until the topping is golden brown and the mango filling is bubbly. Check after about 20 minutes; if the topping is browning too fast, place a piece of aluminum foil on top for the remainder of the baking time. Let the crisp cool for 15 minutes before serving.

Malian Fonio Cakes

These cakes from Mali are baked in muffin tins and can be served as a dessert with fruit, or on their own as a snack. They can be kept covered at room temperature for 1 or 2 days, or refrigerated in an airtight container for up to a week.

INGREDIENTS

2 tablespoons unsalted butter or coconut oil, softened

1 cup fonio flour

1 cup all-purpose flour

1 packet (¼ ounce / 2 ¼ teaspoons) instant yeast

2 cups sugar

1 cup water

2 large eggs

½ cup milk

8 tablespoons unsalted butter, melted, or ½ cup olive oil

2 teaspoons vanilla extract

MAKES ABOUT 20 CAKES

PREPARATION

1. Preheat the oven to 350°F. Grease 20 cups of two standard muffin tins with the softened butter.

2. In a large bowl, combine the fonio flour, all-purpose flour and yeast. In another large bowl, using a whisk, dissolve the sugar in the water. Add the eggs, milk, melted butter, and vanilla and continue whisking until blended. Gradually stir the egg mixture into the flour until combined well. Transfer the dough to a clean work surface and knead until it becomes smooth. Allow the dough to rest for about 30 minutes at room temperature.

3. Press down on the dough to release gas. Divide the dough into 20 portions and place each in a prepared muffin tin cup. Bake for about 20 minutes, until the cakes rise and develop a nice golden top; a toothpick should come out clean when inserted in the center of the cakes.

4. Cool on a wire rack and serve.

Fonio Chocolate Cake with Raspberry Coulis

INGREDIENTS

For Chocolate Cake

¾ cup coconut oil, melted, plus more for greasing the pan(s)

1 cup unsweetened cocoa powder, plus 1 teaspoon for the pan

⅓ cup buttermilk

2 large eggs

4 large egg whites

1 teaspoon vanilla extract

2 cups cooked fonio

1½ cups sugar

1½ teaspoons baking powder

½ teaspoon baking soda

½ teaspoon salt

For the Raspberry Coulis

1 pound fresh raspberries, plus more for garnish

Honey

Powdered sugar, for garnish

SPECIAL EQUIPMENT
12-cup Bundt cake pan or two 8-inch round or square cake pans

MAKES 1 LARGE (9.75 INCH) BUNDT CAKE OR TWO 8-INCH LAYERS

This size cake usually serves 8 to 12 people, but because it is so flavorful, I suggest cutting it into 24 pieces, one per serving. The cake will keep well, refrigerated in a sealed container, for up to 1 week.

PREPARATION

1. Prepare the cake: Preheat the oven to 350°F. Lightly grease a Bundt pan or two 8-inch round or square cake pans with oil. Sprinkle about 1 teaspoon cocoa inside the greased pan(s) to prevent the cake from sticking.

2. In a food processor or blender, combine the buttermilk, eggs, egg whites, and vanilla. Add the fonio and coconut oil and blend until smooth. In a large bowl, whisk together the sugar, cocoa, baking powder, baking soda, and salt. Add the contents of the blender and mix until just combined.

3. Pour the batter into the prepared pan(s). Bake on the center rack for about 50 minutes (or 40 to 45 minutes for the smaller pans), until a knife inserted in the center comes out clean. Remove the cake(s) from the oven and cool completely in the pan(s).

4. Prepare the coulis: Purée the raspberries in a blender. Pass the purée through a fine-mesh sieve; discard the seeds. If you like, sweeten with honey to taste.

5. Turn out the cake(s) onto a serving platter. Dust with powdered sugar and drizzle with the coulis. Slice and serve, garnished with fresh raspberries.

Chocolate & Coconut Pudding with Raspberries

INGREDIENTS

2   cups full-fat coconut milk, plus more as needed

1   teaspoon vanilla extract

½   cup Medjool dates, pitted

½   cup raw cacao powder, plus more for sprinkling

    Pinch of fine sea salt

1   cup cooked fonio

2   tablespoons chopped cocoa nibs or dark chocolate

2   cups fresh raspberries

1   tablespoon toasted unsweetened shredded coconut

SERVES 4

PREPARATION

1. Bring 1 cup of the coconut milk to a simmer in a saucepan. Add the vanilla and turn off the heat.

2. Put the remaining 1 cup coconut milk in a blender. Add the dates, cacao powder, and salt and blend on high until smooth and creamy. Transfer to a large bowl. Fold in 1/2 cup of the vanilla-coconut milk. Add the fonio and fold until well combined. Fold in the remaining 1/2 cup vanilla coconut milk. Gently fold in the cocoa nibs.

3. Refrigerate the pudding for at least 30 minutes to firm up. It should have the texture of chocolate mousse. If it's too firm to serve, stir in more coconut milk.

4. Serve cold with fresh raspberries, a sprinkle of cacao powder, and toasted coconut.

Fonio Porridge with Baobab, Peanuts & Coconut (Ngalakh)

INGREDIENTS

1 cup full-fat coconut milk

1 cup sugar

¼ cup unsweetened smooth peanut butter

2 tablespoons baobab leaf powder (lalo)

1 teaspoon vanilla extract

Pinch of freshly grated nutmeg

2 cups cooked fonio

½ cup raisins (optional)

Crushed peanuts and toasted unsweetened shredded coconut, for garnish

SERVES 4

This is the dish that Christians in Senegal prepare for Good Friday and offer to their Muslim neighbors as a sign of love. It is traditionally prepared with millet couscous. I particularly love this fonio version with the addition of coconut milk.

PREPARATION

1. In a large saucepan, bring the coconut milk to a boil. Reduce the heat to a simmer. Add the sugar and peanut butter and stir until both are dissolved. Add the baobab powder and stir well. Stir in the vanilla and nutmeg, then turn off the heat. Stir in the fonio. Allow the mixture to cool.

2. Stir in the raisins (if using). Divide the porridge among four bowls. Garnish with peanuts and coconut and serve.

Ngalakh Crème Brûlée with Fonio, Baobab & Peanut Butter

This is the custard version of the preceding porridge. Here it becomes a crème brûlée when you caramelize the top with brown sugar, which can be prepared ahead of time and finished with a torch right before serving. It is also okay to serve it without the burnt sugar on top. In that case, I garnish it with toasted coconut and crushed peanuts for a crunchy texture.

PREPARATION

1. Preheat the oven to 300°F.

2. In a large saucepan, bring the coconut milk to a boil. Reduce the heat and add the peanut butter. Mix until well dissolved. Add the baobab powder and mix until well combined. Stir in the vanilla and nutmeg and turn off the heat. Allow the mixture to cool.

3. In a large bowl, whisk the egg yolks with the granulated sugar until the mixture lightens and becomes foamy. Gradually add the coconut milk mixture and whisk vigorously to blend.

4. Divide the fonio among six ramekins. Pour the custard over the fonio. Place the ramekins on a baking sheet and bake for 1 hour. The texture should be firm and set; a toothpick inserted in the center should come out dry.

5. Allow to cool to room temperature. Transfer the ramekins to the refrigerator and chill for 2 hours to set the custard.

6. If you want a sugar crust, sprinkle the tops of the crèmes brûlées evenly with brown sugar. Using a torch, melt the sugar to form a crisp, caramelized top. Alternatively, you can broil the crèmes brûlées for a few minutes. If you choose this option, place the ramekins in the freezer for 15 to 20 minutes before caramelizing. Serve before the sugar crust starts to soften.

INGREDIENTS

- 2   13.5-ounce cans full-fat coconut milk
- ¼   cup unsweetened smooth peanut butter
- 2   tablespoons baobab leaf powder (lalo)
- 1   teaspoon vanilla extract

  Pinch of freshly grated nutmeg
- 5   large egg yolks
- 1   cup granulated sugar
- 2   cups cooked fonio
- 2   tablespoons brown sugar, for the crust (optional)

  Crushed peanuts and toasted unsweetened shredded coconut, for garnish (optional)

SPECIAL EQUIPMENT
Six 3 ½ or 4-inch flameproof ramekins
Kitchen torch

SERVES 6

Fonio Fruit Compotes with Mango or Raspberries

INGREDIENTS

1   pound fresh or frozen
    mangoes or raspberries

2   tablespoons honey or
    brown sugar

    Pinch of salt

3–4 cups cooked fonio

SERVES 4

Compotes are really easy to prepare. They are just like a fruit sauce, and a great way to make use of extra fresh fruits that you may have on hand. Frozen fruits work beautifully, too. Compotes can be stored, covered, in the refrigerator for up to 10 days.

PREPARATION

1. If you're using fresh mangoes, peel them and cut them into 2-inch chunks. With raspberries, leave them whole. If you're using frozen fruit, no need to defrost or slice.

2. In a saucepan, combine the fruit, honey, and salt. Bring to a boil over medium-high heat, stirring occasionally. Cook fresh fruit for about 5 minutes or frozen fruit for 10 minutes, until the fruit has softened.

3. Reduce the heat to medium. Mash the fruit with a fork until it is almost smooth. Continue simmering, stirring often, until the compote has reduced by half, about 5 minutes more. Remove from the heat and let cool for a few minutes before serving with the fonio.

Pineapple & Coconut Clafoutis

INGREDIENTS

2 ½ cups finely chopped pineapple (fresh or canned), drained

6 tablespoons granulated or brown sugar

2 large eggs, separated

⅓ cup fonio flour

3 tablespoons unsalted butter, melted

Grated zest of 2 limes

7 tablespoons full-fat coconut milk

SERVES 6

In this easy-to-prepare dessert, you can substitute the pineapple with cherries, mangoes, or peaches. I love it topped with vanilla ice cream.

PREPARATION

1. In a 3-quart baking dish, stir together the pineapple and 3 tablespoons of the sugar. Set aside to macerate.

2. Heat the oven to 375°F.

3. In a bowl, whisk together the egg yolks and the remaining 3 tablespoons sugar until light and fluffy. Gradually whisk in the fonio flour and melted butter. Add the lime zest and coconut milk and continue to whisk until well combined.

4. In a separate bowl, whisk the egg whites until they form soft peaks. Fold the egg whites into the fonio mixture. Pour the batter over the pineapple.

5. Bake for about 35 minutes, until a toothpick inserted in the middle of the clafoutis comes out clean. Allow to cool to room temperature before serving.

DRINKS

Fonio Milk

In addition to being refreshing and nutritious, homemade fonio milk is easy to prepare. The Medjool dates give it a hint of sweetness. Store in a sealed container in the fridge for up to 4 days.

INGREDIENTS

1   cup cooked fonio
3   cups water
4   Medjool dates, pitted
¼   teaspoon ground
     cinnamon

MAKES 4 CUPS

PREPARATION

1. Blend the fonio with the water until almost smooth. Strain the mixture using cheesecloth or a fine-mesh sieve. Pour the fonio milk back into the blender, add the dates and cinnamon, and blend well. Chill before serving.

Fonio Milk Chai

INGREDIENTS

     Seeds from 6
     cardamom pods
2   whole cloves
4   whole black
     peppercorns
¼   teaspoon fennel seeds
1   cinnamon stick, broken
1   cup Fonio Milk
     (page 148)
½   teaspoon ground ginger
     Pinch of salt
1   cup water
2   teaspoons black
     tea leaves
1   tablespoon honey

SERVES 2

PREPARATION

1. In a spice grinder, combine the cardamom, cloves, peppercorns, fennel, and cinnamon stick and coarsely grind. Combine the spice mix and fonio milk in a small saucepan. Add the ground ginger and salt. Bring to a simmer and cook for 10 minutes on low heat to infuse the milk.

2. Meanwhile, boil the water in a separate pan. Turn off the heat and add the tea leaves. Brew for 5 minutes.

3. Mix the spiced milk and tea together and stir in the honey. Reheat over low heat until hot. Strain through a fine-mesh strainer into two tea cups and serve.

Fonio Beer (Tchapalo)

INGREDIENTS

4   cups raw fonio, rinsed
     and drained well

2   quarts distilled water

6   makrut lime leaves

1½   cups sugar, plus more
     as needed

SPECIAL EQUIPMENT
High-powered blender such
as a Vitamix

MAKES ABOUT 2 QUARTS

This is the traditional method of preparing fonio beer, inspired by my aunt Estelle-Genevieve Soukpo Thiam, who is originally from Benin. Other methods include germinating the fonio grains before blending, but this one is the quickest. In countries like Benin or Burkina Faso, this is the local beverage used for traditional rituals. The sugar takes some of the bitterness off; this will keep for up to 2 weeks, refrigerated, in a glass container.

PREPARATION

1. In a large glass bowl or other glass container, soak the fonio in the water for 1 to 2 days at room temperature, away from the sun, covered with a cheesecloth. The grains should feel pasty in your hands.

2. Working in batches if necessary, put the fonio mixture in a blender and blend well. Return it to the original bowl and cover with a clean cheesecloth. Allow to ferment for 2 more days, away from the sun. The mixture should have a strong but pleasant fermented flavor.

3. Line a fine-mesh sieve with cheesecloth and strain the liquid into a large pot. Add the lime leaves and sugar and bring to a boil over high heat. Reduce the heat to medium and boil for 1 hour, until fragrant. Adjust the flavor with more sugar if you like. Strain through several layers of cheesecloth and refrigerate in glass jars. Serve chilled.

Lisa's Fonio, Papaya & Berries Smoothie

INGREDIENTS

¼   cup cooked fonio

1   small ripe banana, peeled, sliced, and frozen

5   frozen strawberries

     Juice of 1 lime

½   cup orange juice, plus more as needed

½   cup coconut water, plus more as needed

1   tablespoon honey

¼   cup cashew nuts

2   tablespoons unsweetened coconut flakes, toasted (optional)

SERVES 4

My partner, Lisa, prepares this delicious breakfast smoothie. It is creamy, fruity, coconutty, healthy, and delicious. It has a nice crunchy texture from being only partially blended after adding the cashews. You can freeze any leftovers into popsicles for a refreshing treat.

PREPARATION

1. In a blender, combine the fonio, banana, strawberries, lime juice, orange juice, coconut water, and honey. Blend until creamy and smooth, adding more orange juice or coconut water if it is too dense to blend. Taste and adjust the flavor as needed, adding more honey for sweetness or lime for acidity.

2. Add the cashew nuts and pulse a few times to keep the crunchy texture. Pour into tall glasses and garnish with the toasted coconut (if using). Serve immediately.

Mbadiala Cissokho (baby) & Yama Ndiaye

Portraits of Fonio Producers

Adam Bartos' dignified portraits on the following pages pay homage to the true heroes of fonio production. They are the farmers, cooperative workers, temps, and home cooks without whom there would be no fonio in our bowls.

Clockwise from top left: Oumy Haidara, Fantou Demba, Khady Faty, Bana Dabo

Clockwise from top left: Sountou Cissé, Malang Cissé, Sounkar Fadera, Dieynaba Ka

Clockwise from top left: Kémo Daffé, Sira Nanko, Bintou Dramé, Yakaré Keita

Clockwise from top left: Fatou Diop, Mama Djité Dabo, Sadio Dabo, Ndeye Dramé

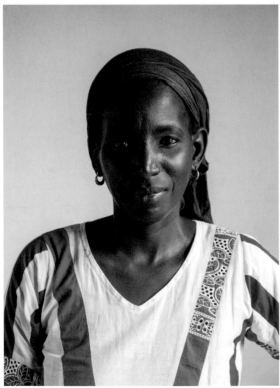

Clockwise from top left: Sékou Daffé, Mariama Dramé, Fatou Nyabalé Dramé, Dior Cissokho

Boubacar Dramé

Clockwise from top left: Maïmouna Camara, Gnimata Djité, Fatoumata Daffé, Tombon Dabo

Clockwise from top left: Coumba Diane, Fatoumata Diawara, Boubacar Daffé, Khadidiatou Ba

Acknowledgments

There are so many people to thank for this book, it would be too difficult to name them all. However, I would like to first express my gratitude to my wonderful children, Sitoë, Elijah, and Haroun, for always inspiring and patiently supporting me.

To my life partner, Lisa Katayama, for taking the time to read and edit the pages of this book.

To Aya N'diaye and the women of the Koba Club cooperative in Kedougou; to Mame Khary Diene; to agronomist Cheikh Gueye for his dedicated help; and to the RAFF team for their work on fonio; to SOS Sahel and to their director Remi Heymerick for believing and supporting the fonio farmers. A special thank you to my business partner and Yolélé cofounder Philip Teverow, for crashing my lamb-roasting party.

To my business partner at Teranga, Noah Levine, for being an early fonio convert. To Emeka Okafor for inviting me—and fonio—onto the TED Global stage.

Thank you also to the Yolélé Foods team, Claire Alsup, Maliha Adams, and all of our brilliant fellows, who have taken up the fonio mission with passion and determination.

To Adam Bartos, my longtime friend, for traveling with me to capture these beautiful photos.

And last but not least, to my publisher Hiroko Kiiffner and to Diana Kuan and Suzanne Fass who patiently edited the many iterations of this book.

Resources

Here is a selection of online stores where you can purchase fonio and other West African ingredients. You can also check the local stores in your area for many of these ingredients.

Amazon www.amazon.com

Gold Coast Supermarket 381 Canal Place, Bronx, NY
www.goldcoastsupermarket.com

Jalé www.jale.co

Kalustyan's 123 Lexington Avenue, New York, NY
www.foodsofnations.com

My African Mart www.myafricanmart.com

Owa Afrikan Market www.owamarket.com

Sahadi's 187 Atlantic Ave, Brooklyn, NY
www.sahadis.com

Wazobia African Market www.wazobia.market

Yolélé Foods www.yolelefoods.com

Bibliography

Amadou , I., M. Gounga, and G.-W. Le. "Millets: Nutritional Composition, Some Health Benefits and Processing: A Review." *Emirates Journal of Food and Agriculture* 25, No. 7 (May 2013): 501-8.

Barikmo I., F. Ouattara, and A. Oshaug. "Protein, Carbohydrate and Fibre in Cereals from Mali: How to Fit the Results in a Food Composition Table and Database." *Journal of Food Composition and Analysis* 17 (2004): 291–300.

Bond. B., et al. "Fatty Acid, Amino Acid and Trace Mineral Analysis of Three Complementary Foods from Jos, Nigeria." *Journal of Food Composition and Analysis* 18, No. 7 (November 2005): 675–90.

Burkill, H. M. *The Useful Plants of West Tropical Africa*, 2nd ed., Vol. 2, *Families E-I.* Kew, Richmond, UK: Royal Botanic Gardens, 1994.

Carbenier, R., P. Jaeger, and F. Busson. "Study of the Protein Fraction of Fonio, *Digitaria exilis* (Kippist) Stapf, a Protein Exceptionally Rich in Methionine." *Annales de la Nutrition et de l'Alimentation* 14 (1960): 165–69.

Chukwu, Ogbonnaya, and Aminat Joy Abdul-kadir. "Proximate Chemical Composition of Acha (*Digitaria exilis* and

Digitaria iburua) Grains." *Journal of Food Technology* 6, No. 5 (2008): 214–16.

Fernandez D.R., et al. "Fatty Acid, Amino Acid, and Trace Mineral Analyses of Five Weaning Foods from Jos, Nigeria." *Plant Foods for Human Nutrition* 57 (Fall 2002): 257–74.

Fogny-Fanou N., et al. "Consumption of and Beliefs about Fonio (*Digitaria exilis*) in Urban Area in Mali." *African Journal of Food, Agriculture, Nutrition and Development* 9, No. 9 (2009): 1927–44.

Food and Agriculture Organization, World Health Organization, and United Nations University Expert Consultation. *Protein and Amino Acid Requirements in Human Nutrition*. Geneva: United Nations, 2002.

Irving, D.W., and I.A. Jideani. "Microstructure and Composition of *Digitaria exilis Stapf* (Acha): A Potential Crop." *Cereal Chemistry* 74, No. 3 (May 1997): 224–28.

Jideani, I.A. "*Digitaria exilis* (Acha/Fonio), *Digitaria iburua* (Iburu/Fonio) and *Eluesine coracana* (Tamba/Finger Millet): Non-Conventional Cereal Grains with Potentials." *Scientific Research and Essays* 7, No. 45 (19 November 2012): 3834–43.

———. "Traditional and Possible Technological Uses of *Digitaria exilis* (Acha) and *Digitaria iburua* (Iburu): A Review." *Plant Foods for Human Nutrition* 54, No. 4 (1999): 363–74.

Jideani, I.A., R.K.O Apenten, and H.G. Muller. "The Effect of Cooking on Proteins from Acha (Digitaria exilis) and Durum Wheat." *Journal of the Science of Food and Agriculture* 65 (August 1994): 465–76.

Jideani, I.A., and V.A. Jideani. "Development on the Cereal Grains Digitaria exilis (Acha) and *Digitaria iburua* (Iburu)." *Journal of Food Science and Technology* 48, No. 3 (June 2011): 251–59.

Kahane, Rémi, et al. "Agrobiodiversity for Food Security, Health and Income." *Agronomy for Sustainable Development* 33, No. 4 (October 2013): 671–93.

Kam, Jason, et al. "Dietary Interventions for Type 2 Diabetes: How Millet Comes to Help." *Frontiers in Plant Science* 7 (27 September 2016): 1454

National Research Council. "Fonio (Acha)" in *Lost Crops of Africa, Volume I, Grains*. Washington, DC: National Academies Press, 1996: 59–75.

Obilana, A. Babatunde, and Eric Manyasa. "Millets." in *Pseudocereals and Less Common Cereals*, edited by Peter S. Belton and John R.N. Taylor. New York: Springer, 2002: 177–217.

O'Kennedy, M.M., A. Grootboom, and P.R. Shewry. "Harnessing Sorghum and Millet Biotechnology for Food and Health." *Journal of Cereal Science* 44, No. 3 (November 2006): 224–35.

Philip, T.K., and I.N. Itodo. "Acha (*Digitaria* spp.), a 'Rediscovered' Indigenous Crop of West Africa." *Agricultural Engineering International: CIGR Journal* 7 (December 2006)

———. "Demographic Characteristics, Agricultural and Technological Profile of Acha Farmers in Nigeria." *Agricultural Engineering International: CIGR Journal* 14, No. 1 (2012): 89–93

Saleh, Ahmed S.M., et al. "Millet Grains: Nutritional Quality, Processing, and Potential Health Benefits." *Comprehensive Reviews in Food Science and Food Safety* 12, No. 3 (8 April 2013): 281–95.

Sarita, Ekta Singh. "Potential of Millets: Nutrients Composition and Health Benefits." *Journal of Scientific and Innovative Research* 5, No. 2 (2016): 46–50.

Sartelet, H. et al. "Flavonoids Extracted from Fonio Millet (*Digitaria exilis*) Reveal Potent Antithyroid Properties." *Nutrition* 12, No. 2 (February 1996): 100-106.

Shahidia, Fereidoon, and Anoma Chandrasekara. "Millet Grain Phenolics and Their Role in Disease Risk Reduction and Health Promotion: A Review." *Journal of Functional Foods* 5, No. 2 (April 2013): 570–81.

Taylor, John R.N., Tilman J. Schober, and Scott R. Bean. "Novel Food and Non-Food Uses For Sorghum and Millets." *Journal of Cereal Science* 44, No. 3 (November 2006): 252-71.

Temple V.J., and J.D. Bassa. "Proximate Chemical Composition of Acha (*Digitaria exilis*) Grain." *Journal of the Science of Food and Agriculture* 56, No. 4 (January 1991): 561–63.

Vodouhe, S.R., A. Zannou, and E. Achigan-Dako, eds. *Proceedings of the 1st Workshop on Genetic Diversity of Fonio (*Digitaria exilis *Stapf), August 1998.* Rome, Italy: Food and Agriculture Organization of the United Nations, 2003, 4-6.

Index